GET READY TO LAUGH

YOUR ASS OFF

Early Praise From My 50's Crowd

"Real life can be so funny, especially in the retelling."

"I can't read these at work anymore! I am the only woman here and these men want to know what is so funny in my office!"

"What a hoot! I needed a good laugh this morning."

"Your no nonsense, matter of fact approach to a natural and normal part of life is refreshing. We are all so up tight about this subject."

"Again, I laughed till my sides hurt. I look forward to your stories, they make my day!"

"You bawdy, ballsy broad! Laughed me arse off!"

"I love, love, love your writing! I laughed all the way through it!"

"This was the perfect thing for me to see at the end of my day. HUGE BELLY LAUGH!"

"It is amazing how many things that are so true in your own life can be so funny when someone else talks about the same things happening! Thanks!"

"Fresh, fresh, fresh, honest, and funnier than shit! Thanks."

"I just laughed so damn hard I woke up both my husband and my dog!"

"I totally cracked up while reading this, and I needed a laugh today."

"I was laughing so much the guys I work with thought I was losing it!"

"I thought I was the only one who held conversations with myself!"

"This gave me a much-needed laugh!"

"I laughed out loud...something I needed!"

"Thanks for sharing, I had to send this to all my girlfriends!"

"You know I love your writing, busted! This is so good, a riot!"

"Ha! Ha! Ha! Ha! Tears!"

"You poor baby, make sure you keep putting it all down, love it!"

"You are funny, very funny."

"You're a riot!"

"I don't think I can read your posts anymore, they

exhaust me!"

"Oh Lord. I am laughing. This is real. This is good. Totally you."

"Oh crap, I just laughed like a really loud loon again."

"Giggles all around, and tears of laughter!"

"OMG!! You are sooo funny!"

"Thanks for the chuckle."

"Hilarious!!!!"

"Turn off the TV, get out of Hollywood and join a Vagina Monologue Tour!"

WHAT'S IN STORE FOR YOU

I guess there's just no denying that age changes us, remolds us, and sometimes leads us to the place where every quiver, every step, shows our ability to transform jam into Jell-O.

~//~

What I hated most about my trainer was, when I'd start moaning and grunting like a pig during our weight lifting sessions, he'd take his fingers and strum the fat on the underside of my upper arm like a virtuoso harp player just to make his point.

~//~

With so many things to already worry about in order to have a somewhat reasonable appearance, the last thing I ever thought I'd have to worry about is VD.

BITCH PLEASE!

VOLUME 1

JACQUI BROWN

BITCH PLEASE!

COPYRIGHT @2011 JACQUI BROWN

FOR PERMISSION YOU MAY CONTACT THE AUTHOR AT: JACQUI@JACQUIBROWN.COM

ISBN-13: 978-1475202403
ISBN-10: 1475202407

BOOK AND COVER DESIGN: JBLA PUBLISHING
PRINTED IN THE UNITED STATES OF AMERICA

TO ALL THE FABULOUS WOMEN IN
THE WORLD WHO HAVE REACHED
THAT WONDERFUL
PLACE IN LIFE WE CALL
THE CHANGE!

DEDICATION

I dedicate this book to all the fabulous, wonderful, stable, unstable, wacky, overworked, underpaid, overstressed, and hormonally disturbed women of the world. In other words—YOU!

It's for those of you who are navigating wildly through the fog of spousal hood, parent hood, mid-life hood, and life in general, but mostly—the biggest life sucking mind fucker of all—MENOPAUSE!

If you're already there, then you know what a wonderful adventure this can be!

I know what you're thinking if you're one of those floundering through this tumultuous time—I'm preaching to the choir, right?

Well maybe I am because some things just have to be said—sometimes out loud! Sometimes louder than other things!

During this wondrous time, many of us take things far too seriously.

Fact is—we should actually be laughing our asses off at every opportunity, at every stupid thing that crosses our path, at every wrinkle that furrows our brow.

Why?

Because we aren't getting any younger!

The insanity of life unfolding the way it does as we muddle through this maze of madness called mid-life, is enough to push us over the edge, off the cliff, in front of a moving train, or straight to our doctors office for a chemical alteration.

Many of us at different times in our lives feel completely insane, inadequate, lost, undermined, over worked, over whelmed, over weight, over budget, over our head, overly bitchy, under appreciated, grossly disrespected and just plain old frustrated!

In retrospect, this could actually be due to the fact that we're always walking around with a little pee on our underwear.

I for one am bloody tired of carrying a small wad of mini-pads in my purse in case I laugh/sneeze/cough, or simply wait too long to get to a bathroom.

Sometimes, we miss the fact that what we should really be doing is giving ourselves a pat on the back for getting here alive and kicking, all while dealing with more than our share of crap.

We juggle!
We jiggle...
Oh crap do we jiggle!
Just ask Ms. Double Chin, Ms. Muffin Top and Ms. Wanna-Be Celebrity look alike Ass!

We rant and rave, scream and yell, sweat and swell, and the whole time—we're feeling utterly out of control.

We pretend that we can do our lives unscathed.

Well I say B.U.L.L.S.H.I.T!

I say it here and now for all of you who won't say it for yourself.

Almost always, we women make do with what we have because sometimes—we don't have any choice.

We persevere in all of our endeavors no matter what, no matter how hard the struggle is, because that's just the way the wind blows, the way the mop flops, the way...oh hell...it just bloody is what it is sometimes!

We sweat, we toil, we sacrifice, and we do it all with a freaking smile on our face.

Yep!

We've got the mother of all game faces and we wear it well.

To each and every one of you, I raise my glass (again and again)!

I toast you for your stamina and tenacity.

I toast you for your capacity to hang on to the end of that rope in order to make it through this wild and most often challenging time we're traveling through.

I hope you will see in the following stories that we women must poke fun at life because that's what keeps us united.

Yeah, I know, you all thought it was because we finally ousted our granny panties and switched to thongs, but the truth is, we're all just sisters—plain and simple.

We live our lives the best we can, with what we have, and we manage it with or without the aid of mind-altering substances (sometimes).

The one thing I know down to my very core, is that we must never, ever, lose our ability to laugh at ourselves or the ridiculous situations we sometimes find ourselves in because if we do—

Well—

We're just not going to let that happen now are we?

Bon Appetite Girlfriends!

Acknowledgements

First and foremost, I want to assure you that no animals, husbands, friends, distant relatives, or children were harmed in the creation of this book. At least that's what I am going to lead you to believe! My lawyer tells me otherwise, but what does he know!

They've all served in some way or another as my inspiration and motivation for penning the following stories. Without them, well, I guess it would be fair to say, I wouldn't have had anyone to poke fun at except myself and that would obviously suck.

It goes without saying that misery loves company so I need to take prisoners along the way.

Secondly, I would like to thank my wonderful, sweet, loving, crazy ass mother. Although she did not pass along the green thumb, something I've always considered her most selfish act (my garden will confirm this), she did give me something far more important. She allowed me to explore my great sense of wonder and appreciation for life. I'm sure there were times when she regretted this decision.

My mom is, you know, special! Even at 80-years-old. She still rocks it.

No matter who hands her lemons, she always manages to come up with the best damned recipe for lemonade, a drink she will generously share often and with everyone, even though alcohol has to be added sometimes to off the problem!

She taught me to live with tenacity, and to endure anything that comes my way. If you've read any of my previous books, you'd know there was a crap load of stuff to endure.

Whatever...

She always allowed me enough rope to let my spirit soar, even when she knew there was a good possibility that I'd crash and burn, or worse, hang myself, which often times ended up to be the case.

I guess today's term for how she treated us was love, tough love. Really tough love!

What I'm mostly grateful for though, is that she gave me the strength to get through things no woman/parent should go through. Yes, she's always had that incredible ability to bitch slap you even when she's holding your hand in sympathy. She may be a short little spud, but boy does she pack a punch. You rock Mom and I love you to death!

Thirdly, I would like to thank my mentor, the late, great Erma Bombeck. Her wit and witticisms have always entertained my warped little brain. You always said it like it was, and I hope that my version of the truth will make you laugh! I hope they have books in heaven Erma!

I must also thank my husband for standing by me during those times (and there were a crap load of times) that tested our ability to keep our sense of humor, our sense of moderate decorum, and our sense of living this fabulous life we're living.

From tears to cheers, all the way down to morning boners, you have always been my cock...I mean my rock! You're the only one brave (or stupid) enough to pick my sorry ass up when I fall and can't get vertical again. I do so love you!

I suppose I have to thank my children as well. Without them life would never have unfolded in such a comical, sometimes mind-blowing epic way, although I think it's quite possible that I might have retained more brain cells without all the aggravation of raising them in today's world.

I should also send a shout out to a few of my girlfriends for letting me blow off steam here and there. Without you I would've had no other choice but to hold someone down with a pillow over their face.

So please enjoy!

It's possible the by the time you finish this book someome may have had me committed, but do send me a note. I'm sure the psychiatric ward is allowed e-mail. Just so you don't have to search for my address I'll post it here.

jacqui@jacquibrown.com

It

Begins...

MENOPAUSE TALK

FRIEND

WHAT WAS THAT SOUND?

ME

WHAT SOUND?

FRIEND

THAT SWISHY SOUND.

ME

OH, THAT'S MY VAGINA.

FRIEND

YOUR VAGINA?

ME

YEAH. MY VAGINA'S SO DRY…

EVERY TIME I WALK INTO A ROOM,

PEOPLE JUST ASSUME I'M WEARING

CORDUROYS!

*I*NTRODUCTION

*H*ow It All Began...

I guess the only place to start this cathartic, if not brilliant decathlon of wisdom, wit, and weirdness is somewhere around the beginning of time...mine that is.

I hate to think about this too much because, well, that was a hell of a long time ago!

There's nothing like a little time to help you develop your survival tactics, your wit, and your ability to laugh under the worst of circumstances.

I was born to parents who, according to my mother, married young as a means of escaping their own painful lives.

My father had just returned from the 'great war' where he stole my mother away from a home where love and abundance were not exactly the talk of the day as she tells it. As a matter of fact, my mother's feeling of loneliness and abandonment, provided by a mother that did not necessarily like children all that much, was basically the catalyst for their union.

My mom married this young handsome soldier, and together they forged their way out into the world. They packed up whatever possessions they had, which was a whole lot of nothing, and moved far far from home to further their escape from parental control.

In 1952 my oldest sister, the calm, cool and collected 'first' child was born. (Sorry girl, your secrets out!) It was shortly after that my mother began to get that telltale inkling in her gut.

According to her, it was not that weird gaseous feeling that often plagues us as we get older, it was more a notion that something was terribly wrong. Something not so fabulous was boiling away on the back burner in regards to her marriage. All she could do at that time was wait and see what would transpire.

It became very apparent as the years rolled by that something major had changed—she was *not* a happy camper!

In 1954 my 'next big sister' popped into the world all googly and gangly. (Yeah, your secrets not safe any more either!) She was the one who always had the *'more stupider than mine'* crooked bangs. My mother used to put a quarter in our pockets and then send us off to the local hairdresser on our trusty little bikes.

Betty M was not so gifted in the hairdressing world, but she was cheap, and she was the only hairdresser in town, so it's not like we had a choice. She had a knack for clipping and snipping our tangled manes into something that resembled that glorious bowl cut that was so famous back then. The beauty of her haircut was that she would, on purpose, cut our bangs on an angle so they would always look like we'd actually combed our hair over. This meant we were stuck wearing our part on the same side until our bangs grew back in. Maybe this is how I got stuck sporting the same basic hairstyle for the past thirty years!

Looking back on that time, I now appreciate the pixie cut we eventually progressed to. It was short, easy to manage, and there were no oddities about it. It was also a huge eye opener because it was then we discovered none of us would have to pony up to have our ears pinned back later in life.

I finally entered the world in or around, um, let's just say, ah, 1956. Oh whatever...Shut Up! What a fine year that was, at least in my opinion it was. My mother, an avid reader, aptly named me after the famous Valley Of The Dolls author,

Jacqueline Susann. No wonder I ended up moving to Hollywood only to become a writer later in life.

I DIGRESS...

I thought I'd struck gold because I was the baby of the family, and we all know what that means. I'd be the one to get spoiled rotten, the one to get everything I wanted. The sun would shine only on me. I'd be the only one who was doted upon by both my parents and my siblings. Did I take advantage of this wondrous time?

YOU BET YOUR BLOODY LIFE I DID!

I milked those years for all they were worth. I went places my sisters couldn't, even though there was really no place that great to go on the kind of budget my parents had to work with. But still, it was something. I was the golden child!

I was (sort of) having the time of my life until, oops, eight years later—my baby sister was born. She was the one that burst my bubble. The straw that broke the camels back. Damn Catholics and their birth control rules! So much for the spoiling shit.

I'd been moved up the ladder to 'half-of-the-middle-child' status. Of course this meant there would be no book ripping my parents a new butt-hole unless my 'other-middle-sister with more stupider bangs than I' was willing to share the load of writing at least half of it.

~///~

I grew up with this weird-ass nickname that no one seems to really know how or why it came into existence. They called me *Kinny*.

What the hell did that mean? Was it an insult? Was it derogatory? Did it mean I was kin, or was it simply that my mother had such a heavy French accent she just couldn't manage the bloody 's' in front of the K. Skinny I could live with. Skinny at least made sense. Skinny would have been brilliant except for the fact that I was always a little roly-poly throughout my early years. Mmm...maybe the *S* was left out for that reason.

All my life I've wondered why they couldn't have come up with something more lyrical like, I don't know, Pumpkin, or Sweetie Pie, or Angel [since I was such a perfect child!] Alas, *'Kinny'* stuck for years and years.

Maybe that was the beginning of the mental foraging I went through in order to uncover my true identity. I grew up in overalls and hand-me-downs. I sported pony and/or pigtails most of the time. I had a split between my front teeth. I had a face full of freckles that seemed to double every summer. That's just the way we rolled back then. How much land, cattle, or pigs you owned, determined your status in the grand little town of Binbrook, Ontario in Canada.

Oh yes, it was grand all right! Aside from the baseball diamonds, which were located at the fair grounds, we also had Armstrong's General Store, a feed mill, and Cybulski's Grocery Store. There was also the little corner store named Bradshaw's. This was where old stupider bangs and I got busted for stealing watermelons one year. Oh yeah. We had this brilliant plan.

We would hide said watermelons up under our shirts and then we'd just casually walk away. There's something about a couple of barely teenaged kids walking along the street, in a town where everyone knew everyone, with belly's that looked literally ripe enough to burst. Pregnancies were never private in our tiny enclave, so it was always a dead giveaway that something was a skitter. Dumb-asses we were! And guess what? Once you're pegged as a fruit thief, you're pegged for life. Maybe that's where my wonderful step-father (papa) came up with his name for us. He used to call us the wit sisters—half-wit, dim-wit, and nit-wit. My baby sister lucked out because she became plain old witless.

Even today, when I walk past the big wooden bin filled with watermelons outside my grocery store, I break a sweat. I'm sure someone's watching me. Usually when they're in season I try to use the store entrance that has someone begging for money rather than be tempted by that old haunting criminal record. I'll be damned if I'm going to jail for something that makes my chin and chest sticky and makes me pee too often!

Something else that was kind of interesting about our little town is that we had an all volunteer fire department. This wouldn't have been so bad had they all looked like the hunky/gorgeous firemen we see today. No, our guys would hear the siren start blasting in the center of town. They'd look up at the sky to see where the smoke was then brush the cow shit off their boots, tuck in their guts and their grimy t-shirts and then they'd jump into their old trucks to head off in the direction of the smoke. Consequently, there were a lot of total rebuilds around town.

We had one cop, Mike, who made a regular run through our sleepy little hollow. We only ever knew him as *Mike the OPP* (Ontario Provincial Police) officer. I don't think anyone ever knew his last name, and I'm not sure why that was, it just was. The only reason I really remember him so well is because he used to bust anyone who went parking (as in making out). He knew every nook and cranny, every stinking hideaway, every little shack where we'd go to have our secret little trysts. 'Big Mike' seemed to have this weird, perfectly timed, internal radar thing. He'd always show up right when you were about to get 'jiggy' with it. His car would roll up to a quiet stop behind your car right at that exact moment your current crush unclasped your bra and was about to round the corner towards second base.

It was the same every time. There'd be that familiar tap on the window, then a few minutes would pass. That's when he'd turn on the flashlight, shine it through the window so he could look inside the car. I believe those precious minutes before he ventured a gander were to allow you enough time to put your clothes back on, sit up, and be presentable and completely cognitive for his standard lecture.

"There are a lot of bad people out there who do bad things…blah, blah, blah, blah, blah!"

"Well, we were just about to do something bad that would be good," is what I always wanted to say, but I knew he wouldn't care. The whole lecture, which he recited like the freaking Miranda Rights, took about seven minutes. When he finished his recitation, he'd just stand there until you started the car and drove away. And just to make sure his message was clear, he'd follow you for a while until you were frustrated enough to call it a night and just go home un-groped, un-sexed, and always with a certain amount of sperm build up powering your date.

I guess in truth, we should've all been grateful he was around because he probably eliminated a lot of unwanted pregnancies during our formative years!

Dr. Bell, the town doctor, had an office in his house, and on occasion we would visit him there. In most cases however, you usually just called him up and a short time later he'd show up at your door with his little black bag tucked neatly up in his armpit.

He and I had a pretty good relationship because I was somewhat of a klutz. (Yes there are parts of my body that read like a roadmap.) If I could fall, or it could fall on me, well, so be it. That's usually how everything seemed to happen. If I could stick my finger in something that usually had an outcome of life threatening injuries—yep—in went the finger.

When we were kids, we rode our bikes everywhere. We didn't have a choice. *Our* parents taught us to be self-reliant. *They* didn't drop everything to schlep us around. If we needed to get further than our legs or bike could propel us, we'd stick out our thumb and hitchhike, otherwise—we didn't go anywhere.

Back in those days hitchhiking was no big deal. We never thought about the worst-case scenario. Hell, we were so dumb back then we didn't even know there was a worst case scenario. Never in our wildest dreams did we imagine some stranger picking us up on the side of the road so they could do bad things to us.

The only *bad things* that filled our minds back then was when mom issued us the standard list of chores. Those were worse than bad. There was plenty of weeding, gardening, hanging clothes on the clothes line, or worse yet, spending the afternoon shoveling shit out of stalls in the neighbors barn so the fucking cows would be comfortable. My sister and I slept in a leaky basement, but by God the neighbor's cows were living La Vida Loca.

That's what we worried about. Not that this *kid stealing* crap wasn't already going on, we just never heard of it. I suppose if we'd had a bloody television early on then we might've clued into this dire statistic. We'd have been more in the know, more aware that the world was bigger than the 2 or so acres that made up our little dot on the map.

Back in the day, if there ever was a parental child abduction, I'll guarantee you, either the husband paid off the wife, or the wife paid off the husband so one or the other could have a little peace and quiet for a few days.

~///~

I've been guilty of doing this myself during the years my children were small. But we did it slightly different, and it wasn't against the law. There were no Amber Alerts flashing along the freeway putting everyone on alert that your lazy ass wanted to sleep in. That you wanted to shirk your parental duties for a day or two, or even a week here and there. No! We paid dearly for our sins. We paid barrels of money to those wonderful, young, overly energetic, camp counselors who seemed tickled pink to have your children under their wing for a day, or a week, or if you were wealthy enough—a month. What the hell was up with those counselors anyway? I don't know if they put something in the juice they drank in the morning to give them all that energy, but I sure as hell wanted what they had for breakfast.

I was always the one standing at the back of the line because I was late. Every morning my car would create a dust bowl as I raced through the gravel parking lot only to slide across the white chalk line just in time. If you were on the other side of that line at the cut off time they came out and gave you that cutesy twirl of the hand that meant you should turn around because no way were they letting your fucking kid in.

I was also always the one who tried to over-compensate for my early morning fucked up Medusa hair by donning oversized Jackie O-esque sun glasses. I'd never have the time to put on regular clothes, so I was always the freaky looking woman who showed up wearing crappy pajama's. And yes, they were the kind that should never have seen the light of day, especially out in public. Now you know two new things about me. I am sometimes late and sometimes lazy, however, I do have my pride and in trying to disguise said pajamas, I'd usually throw on my favorite crappy old black sweater because it hung down to my knees. Funny thing, some people might have thought that sweater quite fashionable if I'd lied and told them it had been macramed. Truth was, it had suffered through several moth infestations and I just never had the heart to throw it out. This was one of those situations where I had to either wear it no matter what anyone said about it, or tie a knot in one end and hang a plant with it.

~///~

We were just young and dumb country bumpkins. I'm sure there were plenty of perversions unfolding all around us but we were oblivious to them.

We didn't watch the news, read the paper, or listen to gossip. That was something the adults did—not us. That was grown up shit!

Well, actually on the gossip end, when we could get away with it, we'd quietly pick up the phone and secretly listen in on our neighbor's conversations. Yes, that was back in the olden days when there were rotary phones and party lines and we all shared airtime. It's amazing what people will say when they think no one else can hear them. We'd discover who was pregnant, who was in jail, who was breaking up, and who was fucking who. It was always interesting to know these things even though we never really gave a damn about them. So long as they weren't talking about us–we didn't care?

Anyway, it was the time in my life when I didn't have to worry about what was coming next, because nothing big really ever happened. The most exciting thing I had access to when I was a youngster was playing baseball. What a glorious time that was. When I stood on that pitchers mound, that worn leather glove wrapped around my hand, OMG! I thought the sun shone only on me. I was in my glory. I'd found my place in the spotlight. I was a super star! Feeling that hard leather ball leave my unfurling fingertips, watching it hurtle towards its destination, was simply nipple hardening.

I had acquired a bit of a reputation for my fabulous, incredible pitching abilities. I'd even gotten a trophy one year that had a pink bubble coming from the lips of the statue. This was a tribute for always having a wad of bubble gum in my mouth during the game. Yep, it was my secret weapon, my sure thing, because it would make the ball arc magically towards its target. Blow a bubble–throw a strike. Those were the days. Wish that trick still worked in real life. Now if I want to blow something, I have to take the gum out of my mouth first!

Growing up in the 50's, 60's and 70's was a rather amazing time. We of course, during that era, had our own version of previous ancient wars, the ones we would eventually learn about in school. We had Vietnam, and we became part of a movement that entailed peace, love, sex, drugs, and rock and roll.

Although I was never into the whole drug thing, so many people drifted in and out of consciousness for nearly a decade until they started figuring out that they were never going to have a life in this fucked up, annihilated state.

Now, you have to remember that Canada was *not* in the war, but because there were so many young men that fled there in order to keep their freedom and stay alive, we felt very much a part of the United States. We would be part of 'the freedom fighters party'. We were 'that place' where young men could migrate, hide out, or escape to in order to reach their 20th, 30th, or hopefully their 80th birthday.

The thing I remember most about all those boys is that they were, for the most part...amazingly gorgeous. Didn't do me a bit of good though, I was still jailbait. This just proves that timing is everything.

Anyway, the 70's came and went in a flurry. When you're in your twenties, time flies as you stumble about trying to discover just who you are and where you're going.

I tried on marriage to my childhood sweetheart. Yep! I hit nineteen and thought I knew it all. Of course, it turned out that I didn't know anything yet and ended up getting divorced a year and a half later. Somehow I could not stay married to a boy who had moved from boyfriend status—to husband status—and then to brotherly status, all inside of one year. As much as we professed to love each other, we both eventually agreed it was time to move on and so we did.

Working and living in a steel town, where fabulous careers were rare or unheard of, just didn't do it for me. It d-u-l-l-e-d me out! Your choice was to work at one of two steel factories, become a nurse [okay, so that's a fabulous career and I would have made a good one I think], or you could work for someone who would reap the benefits of all your hard labor. That was not what I had in mind for myself.

I had dreams, big fucking dreams, and I was not about to squander the rest of my twenties at a dead-end job in a dead-end town.

I took a leap of faith one day, bought a one-way ticket to paradise, and jumped on a plane to sunny California. I knew it was my destiny. I wanted something bigger and better than settling on ho-hum. I did not want that 'have a baby or ten, put on 300 pounds' kind of life.

I admit now, it was a pretty gutsy move on my part because I only had a few hundred dollars to my name. That didn't matter though. Nothing was going to stop me. I had no ties keeping me there other than my family. I had balls. I was fearless. And I was ready to spread my wings and fly!

I was going on an adventure to a new place, with my two suitcases stuffed with every worldly possession I owned, and my wee wad of cash. I was headed to a place where I didn't know a soul.

I COULD START A—BRAND-SPANKING NEW UNCENSORED, UNINHIBITED, DO AND BE ANYTHING I WANT—KIND OF LIFE!

That's the beauty of youth! You think you know everything, know what you're doing, and you're stupid enough to believe it. Yep, that's me! I've always loved to stretch my belief in myself, and that challenge, well, it was right up my alley.

Hell, I've been here in California now for more than thirty-three years, married to the same guy for all these years, with two lovely (insert cough) children, so I guess it's safe to say—things worked out.

So there you go. Now you know how I got here. How my life has unfolded over the past three decades will come in the form of short stories based on my observations about life, love, family, parenting, and whatever else decides to fall out of my brain on the following pages.

Oh…by the way, did I mention I'm menopausal?

It could get dangerous in here!

*N*otes from the

50's...

i mean—my 50's...

One

Funny How...

...we can look at ourselves in the mirror without recognition sometimes. Maybe it's self-preservation. Maybe it's denial. Maybe it's a little of both. Let's face it, we've all had that—gasp—heart pounding, gut wrenching moment, when we realize who's looking back at us in that reflection.

In my book, if you don't acknowledge things like muffin-tops (unless of course you're baking), or back fat (unless you're frying bacon), then they just don't exist. When you get to my age, you learn so many cool tricks to fool yourself into believing that time has been tremendously kind to you.

Unfortunately, we sometimes get caught between that bloody rock and a hard place [the mirror and reality] and we finally have to accept what's there in that reflective surface.

Crap!

So I have to wonder as I always do...who's fooling who? Does everyone else see what I'm in complete denial over?

Just the other day I caught sight of my almost bare ass, and thought to myself, who in their right mind would let something like that go around uncovered?

"Have you no shame girl," I said to myself as I inspected the mid-life 'junk' trying to escape the confines of my brand new panties! Oh...well! I guess this was bound to happen now that I've switched to a thong, but whatever! This probably means I can no longer actually use the term *confines* unless I'm referring only to my butt crack since that's all a thong can manage to confine.

Okay, it's not like I run around naked all the time, although I have to believe my husband would like that since he is, without a doubt, a consummate ass man.

Oh yes! He's been known to shimmy his hand down the back of my pants at the most inopportune time, like on an escalator at the mall, or when I'm standing next to him talking to someone. (This also makes some people think I stutter because I have to adjust to his out of control, icy cold paw mid-sentence.) He'll do it any time he thinks he can get away with it. He is purely evil in this way, but hey, at least I know he still loves my ass.

Thank God for small favors!

Let's just pray he never gets his eyesight checked!

Now let's get one thing straight right now, right here on this page. I would never, ever, on purpose, put myself in the position of watching this—got a life of it's own pearly-white flesh floe—undulate freely.

This was a rather unfortunate sighting. It was an ACCIDENTAL VIEWING. I would never, ever, on purpose, try to hurt my own damn eyes, or my own damn ego.

On occasion I get dressed in the bathroom since my closet doesn't have a heater vent so obviously, accidents like this are bound to happen. [FLAB AND GOOSE BUMPS ARE NOT A GOOD COMBINATION UNDER ANY CIRCUMSTANCES MIRROR OR NOT!]

Now—my b-u-t-t is not a horrific looking thing by any means [self-denial], and it will never be compared to a certain famous celebrity butt, but like everything else, time has proven a worthy opponent.

I remember when I used to go shopping for jeans and never ever once gave the idea of *shaping jeans* a second thought. I didn't have to back in the day because I only had a little junk-in-the-trunk as they call it! You know what I mean?

I proudly flaunted those lovely round chunks of flesh like a peacock strutting its plume of feathers for all to see.

There used to be definite delineations between my butt cheeks and the back of my thighs. I'd never really given any thought about lift and separation in *'that'* area because I'd always believed that you only had to consider that problem when it came to your boobs. Those puppies, well, that's a whole different animal.

Just recently I went to the mall with the sole purpose of buying a new hipper, ripped up, stone washed, gem studded, flesh sucking pair of jeans hoping they would trick the onlookers eye.

Yes, mid-life does this to women, at least to those of us who are trying to hold on to the past in hopes that it will make us better looking people in the future.

WE HAVE TO MAINTAIN SOME KIND OF STANDARDS DON'T WE GIRLS?

The last thing I want is for my kids to accuse me

of wearing frumpy old 'GRANNY' jeans.

Admit it, we've all got at least one pair of those hideous baggy denim's stashed away in our closet somewhere for 'those' days when our excess is apparent. You know the ones I'm talking about. The ones with the elastic waist. The ones with those big old pleats in the front so we can hide that childbearing trophy bulge that protrudes between our crotch and our bellybutton. The same bulge your doctor promised would dissipate when you were breastfeeding. Well, after 24 years, I finally had to give up on that theory because it doesn't always work. Besides, have you ever tried to convince a grown child that nursing is still beneficial to them? No way, Jose! They just look at you dumb-founded and tell you that your fat belly is your problem, not theirs.

Even worse, those granny jeans have those big-ass deep front pockets. They make your problem look even bigger but they do offer one benefit. You'll always have a place to put your boobs once the spring has sprung.

And I'll bet you, if you look hard enough, you'll probably find a few pair of granny underpants to go with them. We used to refer to them as period panties. I'm sure if you look hard enough, you'll find at least one pair sitting right next to your now treasured thongs.

Why have we switched to the butt floss panty some may ask? Well I for one know that they absolutely eliminate that fat separation from your first butt-cheek to the little one that grew just below it. I'll confess right here that my once J-Lo-ish butt has left the building. Who took her place? That would be, no doubt, Sponge Bob Square Pants of course!

Well, as it turns out, those newer, hipper jeans are not always the best for hiding loose flesh. What I discovered as I hid behind the curtain is that spandex, as girdle like as it is, is not always as flattering as it professes to be. Yes, it can take an inch off your thighs, and yes it can push and shove your butt into its correct position after an hour of contorting your legs up and down, but, it also pushes a lot of other things to places you were trying to forget about—i.e: the muffin top!

JUST WHAT I WANT, SOMETHING THAT MAKES THAT EVEN WORSE THAT IT WAS BEFORE!

Another problem with these new jeans is, if you don't happen to be a pubic hair groomer, your belt buckle will always have a little afro. If I ever wanted to dye my hair blonde, this would be a dead give away that I am a true-blue brunette. Who on this bloody earth came up with that one-inch zipper? On a Barbie doll this works perfectly fine because:

1. She's only a little anatomically correct.

2. She's hairless.

3. That bitch has abs of steel.

Perhaps this was the result of doing Ken and G. I. Joe during her rein in the toy industry!

In real life we should be subjected to this?

Get real designers!

There is no fucking way this is going to be enough to hold back our bushel of hair. There is no possibility this wild, dark, out of control hair patch belt buckle is going to blend into my skin tone. On the other hand, it could be one of those entrepreneurial moments. I could actually design a belt buckle, white or black, that had a little face design on it, something along the lines of a surprised 'Mr. Bill'. All you'd have to do is add that little escaped hair patch and voila, you'd have your own 'live' version of a chia pet!

And another thing...

Whose brilliant idea was it to shred the thigh area in the first place? I have to admit, I think it looks pretty damn cool when you're standing up (and you're twenty-something). It's very trendy, however, the moment you sit down and that stretchy denim pulls itself taut against your upper thigh, well, what comes to mind for me is that old play dough machine we used when we were kids that allowed you to make spaghetti.

Your errant flesh pushes through all those loose threads and...yikes! How is it possible that something like that can be considered cool?

I guess there's just no denying that age changes us, remolds us, and sometimes leads us to the place where every quiver, every step, shows our ability to transform jam into Jell-O.

I don't know. The more I think about it, the more I realize that maybe there's something to be said about granny pants after all!

$\mathcal{T}$wo

In Passing...

...gas that is, I've come to the conclusion that every time I let one rip, I'm adding yet another X on my carbon footprint.

That's why I never attend those clever little 'green' conferences. Without a doubt, I'd be the one walking around with the big ass neon sign hovering near my ass that say's "guilty, guilty, guilty". I can hear the announcer now: ATTENTION CONFERENCE ATTENDEES, WE HAVE A PUBLIC FARTER ON THE LOOSE! IF

THERE ARE ANY VENDORS HERE DEMONSTRATING VENTILATING SYSTEMS, WE COULD SURE USE YOUR HELP ON AISLE 12!

I've tried to do my part for the environment. I've been pretty diligent about changing my light bulbs and unplugging appliances, but this internal gas thing seems completely out of my control now.

Age tends to load us up with lots of aches and pains, but from my experience, after you let a cheek-flapping fart loose, many of those aches and pains miraculously disappear.

I swear to God, ninety-nine percent of the time I'm spot on.

I've always been a big believer that everything that ails you boils down to something as simple as gas.

My kids tell me their stomachs hurts.

"Once you fart you'll feel better", I say. "Let her rip."

"But mom!"

"I think I have appendicitis."

"Fart, you'll feel better. Trust me."

"But mom!"

"I think I broke my arm".

"Just fart…oh…wait…maybe we should see the doctor."

I hate it when the little bastards throw a wrench in the engine.

Okay, sometimes it's not gas and you actually have to do something to cure what ails them, but for the most part, it's a pattern children follow as they reach for attention.

In mid-life, I've come to the conclusion that gas is actually one of life's perks as you travel towards that golden era. It's a glorious thing too! We can write off nearly everything that's going on in our body as gas related. Who wants to think of the alternative? I get a chest pain…it damn well better be gas, and guess what…it usually is!

Yes, I tend to live in the mind-set of 'IGNORANCE IS BLISS'. And why the hell shouldn't we think like this? We have so many other things to worry about in this crazy world surrounding us!

When we were kids we never thought too much about farting so why start now? We just let it go whenever back then. We didn't care who heard it. As a matter of fact, the grosser we made it sound the better we felt. It became a job well done! Hell, we even tried to emulate the sound with our hand and armpits just for the hell of it. We would earn credits and kudos from our friends. It was our time of 'the more the merrier'.

Oh yeah, if you could press your butt against

something solid, something that would enable the noise to become this thunderous crescendo, WHOO-HOO!

We used it as a tool to gross out our friends, family, and acquaintances.

We did it in the classroom at school because we knew no one could escape the foul air, especially in the winter because the windows were sealed up due to foul weather. My motto always used to, you want foul weather, I'll give you foul weather my fair weathered friends!

We did it in the car when we knew our parents had the safety locks on the windows so none of us could 'accidentally' fall out of the moving vehicle. We'd let her rip then wait patiently for the aroma to waft forward from the backseat to the front. We'd wait for signs of recognition on our parents faces, and then we'd wait with great anticipation for that age-old question—'who farted'?

"Not me".

"Not me".

"Not me".

It was a game we all played very well.

It was always a giggle inducer though as my sisters and I sat piled on top of one another watching as my mother secretly surveyed my father's face out of the corner of her eye to see if she could detect any signs that he was the culprit. Even if she did suspect him, we knew she'd never say anything because it was never good to embarrass the father in front of the children. She'd just feign a hot flash, ask hubby to unlock the windows, then she crack it down a little and maintain her presumption that it was one of us kids. By the way, my mother was always right in her assumptions!

Why is that father's don't need an excuse for this kind of behavior? They just do as they please and expect everyone to ignore it? There's no *excuse me* or *oops*. It's just a man thing that, when it happens, you somehow manage to ignore it. You diplomatically turn the other cheek, and pray to God they don't turn the other cheek!

Unfortunately for most of us, somewhere along the way we developed this sense of pride and that took all the fun out of it.

If we got gas past the age of twelve, we'd undo a button, open our zipper an inch or two to help relieve the pressure, or we'd suck back some kind of bubbly drink hoping it would diffuse the bubbles in our belly without having to let them pass naturally.

We'd suffer through countless seconds, minutes, or hours until we could find a private place to let our suffering go. We had reached the age where it just wasn't polite to fart in public anymore. We would not be able to deal with the ridicule if we got busted.

It didn't matter how bad you felt holding it in, you just sucked up. You squeezed your butt-cheeks together, and waited until an appropriate time and place arrived where we could undo the evil that lurked within.

On a recent visit to my local grocery store, the one that offers seniors shopping day every Friday, I was inexplicably possessed with joining my elders in their unpretentious symphony of sound.

I showed up at the store with that awful gurgling feeling in my gut. I'd tried to wait it out at home, and had already fired off a few warning shots, but I realized I was running out of time to get all my errands done so off I went. I knew this evil little bastard was skulking about and ready to go, but pride was fighting me tooth and nail. I sucked up, walked up and down the aisles squeezing my cheeks together like I was doing some kind of cardio-muscular Brazilian Butt Lift exercise to improve the look of my ass. And then I prayed to God I could hold on for just a little bit longer. If I could make it to the produce department, then I could blame the airborn foulness on the brussel sprouts or cabbage. Or better yet, if I could make it to the deli section I could let her rip then make a stink of my own, because my store's deli is famous for its rather large bowl of boiled eggs. There's nothing on earth that smells more like a fart than boiled eggs.

But, try as I might, there was no doubt in my

mind that there was no holding this one back. The churning in my gut had become audible to anyone in the near vicinity. This sucker had developed a life of it's own!

I was, in every sense of the word—becoming D.E.S.P.E.R.A.T.E!

On this particular day, there were more people in the store than usual, and most of them seemed to be around my age.

I began searching for that *'golden aisle'*, the one that had a couple of senior citizens ambling along.

I was practically running by this time when I finally, by the grace of God, found my victims! Do you know how hard it is to run when you're squeezing your cheeks together that tightly?

Bingo!

"Hello shoppers, we've got two old farts on aisle ten".

I think by this point my lips were turning blue from trying to hold my breath so nothing could escape from any portal on my body. I believe there was even a tear in my eye as I approached these two unsuspecting old fogies. I'm not sure if the tears were from relief, or from disbelief that I was about to blow and let them take the fall. The fact was, I didn't care at this point.

I managed to maneuver myself between senior

one and senior two. IT WAS SOOOO PERFECT! I reached up and grabbed a can of something from the shelf and pretended to read the label in order to maintain my position. Then I felt 'it' move and prepared myself for release.

Oh yes baby!

There was no sound, thank God, but it took a hell of a lot longer than I'd anticipated to deliver this loaded and lethal weapon.

Out of the corner of my eye I could see one of the seniors slowly approaching my position. Unfortunately, just beyond her, was this very handsome guy (okay, he was fucking gorgeous and the fireman's uniform didn't hurt either) who was also making his way towards ground zero.

"OH CRAP!"

I knew I had to bust a move, so I set the can down and headed directly towards the old woman and Mr. Rub My Nipples Handsome Guy. I knew that if I could get next to that old gal I'd be home free, innocent, off the hook.

Like most things in life, timing is everything.

I got next to her in record time, and because my nose is very sensitive, I knew that foul odor, the beast, had followed me.

I took two steps beyond her, which put me about five feet from Mr. Handsome. He looked my way (yes, he was checking me out) and I immediately went into my thespian-award-winning acting moves.

I grimaced. I pointed my thumb towards the old lady who was now a few feet behind me, and then appropriately waved my fingers under my nose. Then I made that 'whew' expression and kept on moving.

It was going to be okay. I had gotten off scott-free! I was in the clear! The old bag was going to take the heat for this one. As I headed towards the front of the store I heard the old lady cough a few times but I just kept going.

I felt so much better, that much I can tell you. The only thing that worried me was the fact that I'd worn white pants that day and there was a good possibility, due to the intensity of the fart, that I might have left a skid mark, but then I realized I'd worn a reasonably long shirt and that would cover any evidence of said accident.

In the check out line, I stood there waiting for them to slide everything over the scanner. I had accomplished one more chore on the list. Everything was going along perfectly well until, low and behold, both the old bag and Mr. Rip My Clothes Off Now Please Handsome guy got into the same line as me.

Crap!

I tried to ignore them by fussing with my

coupons, but all of a sudden, without any warning, I felt the front of her cart bump into my hip. When I turned to look at her in protest of this physical intrusion I couldn't help but notice this odd look on her face.

"Jesus Christ, you just about bloody killed me back there," she says to me. "Girl, you should take something for that!"

Mr. Handsome Guy is privy to this dialogue of course and starts to laugh uncontrollably. I could actually feel my sphincter muscle trying valiantly to pull itself up inside my body to cover its shame.

I left the store that day vowing that I will never, ever again, pass gas at the grocery store no matter how old I get!

$\mathcal{T}$HREE

Does This Make My...

...ass, gut, back, neck, face, thigh, calves, ankles, arms look fat?

We've probably all been guilty of asking this stupid freaking, self-defeating question once or twice.

What possesses us to ask it in the first place is beyond me because, point in fact, there is only one answer we want to hear–no, no, and NO! Any other answer could lead to, let's just say—a good bit of damage control from whomever must respond.

There can be so many repercussions to this answer, and some of them linger around for a very long time.

Of course this explains why my husband never wants to shop with me. Maybe he's smarter than I think.

The second he hears the words 'does this make'…he's up and out of the room faster than a Daytona race car. God bless him! That man has a survival instinct like no one else I know.

The first thing they teach you in school, if you can remember that far back is…

"IF YOU ALREADY KNOW THE ANSWER, DON'T ASK THE QUESTION!"

…unless of course you really want to put someone in the hot seat. If you, after giving this some thought, still ask the question, then you're dumber than you look and you deserve the truth!

We're not complete idiots about our body image. We know when all of the above looks good or not. We have mirrors! We can see as plain as day when our boobs have fluctuated in size and our cups runneth over. And there's only a certain amount of times we can accuse the dry cleaner of shrinking our pants (again) or altering our shirts so the buttons no longer close (again)!

At this age, most of us are in denial about what's happening to our, for lack of a better word, flesh host.

Yes, sometimes we put the blinders on for self-preservation, but we know. We feel *"it"* move when we walk. This is why I don't run anymore. I do not want my back-fat or ass gyrating and screaming "look at me–look at me" in public places. I figure the slower I move the better I can hide it. If you've ever been in the position of walking behind someone who is, let's just say, well endowed in the ass area, you know it's like watching a giant slinky in motion. It never stops. They have to stand still for several minutes before their flesh settles into just lying there. Just sayin'!

I think the first inkling that change is upon us is when you start to lose those little hollows in your cheeks. You know exactly what I'm talking about. It's that thing that makes your face look like you have those glorious cheek bones, and can often make you appear thinner than you really are. It's flattering and it's youthful.

Unfortunately, when the tides of youth start slipping into middle age, things tend to get lost or buried in the shuffle. When that hollow fills, it means that extra weight is secretly being added while you sleep. (This has absolutely nothing at all to do with the second helping of cheesecake, or the loaf of bread you ate with last night's dinner. No really!!)

This is not good because it also means that jowls are right around the corner.

Yeah! It seems cruel that the face is usually the first place this shows. I'll admit it right now—both my dimples have become buried amid the debris of the passing years. Well actually, the truth is, I just noticed that they're not really gone, they just relocated to my ass.

TRAITORS!

A lot of people judge what's going on with their body by how their clothes fit. This I believe is a really good way to judge your girth because, if they still fit you, even if they're tighter than hell, it's a win-win situation. No gain, no pain! If you can still get the zippers and the buttons to close you're ahead of the game. This of course falls under the category of reverse-reverse-reverse psychology. Think of all the money you'll save not having to shop for skinny clothes or larger (fat) clothes.

I've learned my lesson over the years as my weight fluctuated up and down. I've come to the conclusion that after thirty odd years or so of yo-yo dieting, trainers, boot camps, and starvation, I am never going to lose my baby (pregnancy) fat. As a matter of fact, I don't think I can actually use that term anymore when it comes to those little pudgy spots. (My youngest child is seventeen). The truth of the matter is that this is plain and simple *fat-fat* now.

Yep. This is finally the time in our lives when we have to suck up and admit to ourselves that our M.I.L.F. (Mother I'd Like To Fuck) days are a thing of the past.

I actually held a memorial for myself the day I realized this point in my life had passed. I remember it so vividly. I'd pulled up at the usual spot in front of my daughter's school. It was obvious all the young boys were gathered around her waiting patiently for my arrival. I tooted the horn to get her attention but she was too caught up in conversation to hear the familiar sound of my horn. Instead of just sitting there I decided to get out of my car and cross the street to personally retrieve her. As I approached her I saw the light go on in one boys eyes. Two steps closer, I see the light disappear. It had been replaced with a look of repulsion. I smiled my best smile at him but nothing happened. I flipped my hair back over my shoulder hoping I could dissolve the iciness of his glare but still nothing. What he did do though will be forever etched in my mind. He slaps his pal on the shoulder, then points to me. This makes my daughter realize that someone is standing behind her. She turns around and I can see her eyes go as round as saucers.

What the hell are you wearing, she says to me.

What? I say as I look down at my clothes. OMG! I was still in my dirty, filthy, baggy, disgusting gardening clothes that were reserved solely for wear in my backyard.

I had caused my own demise.

I could hear the boys laughter as they walked away. After that experience I made my daughter walk all the way down the street, ALONE, to a new pick up spot.

I threw my scale out a long time ago because it always betrayed me. I'd strip down to nothing, stand on its hard cold surface, and the little hands would just start spinning out of control as it determined how much it was going to punish me.

Well, I'll bet it really spun out of control as it descended towards the cold hard pavement after I threw it out the second story bathroom window.

BASTARD!

Now don't get me wrong, I'm not hideous, but everything is relative isn't it? When your waist expands it becomes more relative with your hips and your rib cage, as in *if they're the same size, you actually can no longer refer to it as your waist.* It's now considered just another part of your torso, or, as I like to call it my boy shape, my masculine side. This isn't always a bad thing because, if you happen to have a little more junk in the trunk it will no longer stand out on its own. This of course eliminates any of those God-awful references to pears or any other fruit. In my book, this can be a good thing.

What I wonder is, why don't men ask this question? I mean mid-life does the same thing to them so why do they remain silent? How are they able to maintain their calm, cool, and collected demeanor when their belly enters a room before they do? What's their secret? Don't they ever get frustrated when they can't see their toes or their own damned penis anymore?

Could it be that age changes us in different ways? Do they lose their peripheral vision first? Do they see only what they want to see? Or are they simply perfectionists at tomfoolery?

Maybe we should just rip that page out of their book and stick it in ours!

I know plenty of men who've got that belly overhang thing going on. They don't struggle with it as we women do; they just let it all hang out. They stuff it into that shiny brand new red convertable Corvette they just bought and go on their way.

The only time that I know of when it seems to bother them, or they become self-conscious of it, is when they see a beautiful girl—you know the one—we've all seen her. She makes *'it'* move! Suddenly their shoulders go back, their chest puffs out, and three or four inches of flab suddenly disappears from their waistline.

Maybe the question "does this make my (insert body part) look fat" should be banned from public usage like they did with the 'N' word. Maybe it should go the way of the bible or any reference to God—out of schools, out of political offices, and into the 'silence is golden' ruling!

Oh well, I guess time has a way of doling out these little wake up calls just to keep us on our toes, or at the very least, able to see our toes most of the time!

Speaking of muffin(top)—I have to run—the timer just went off on the oven.

I think my brownies, I mean...my roasted vegetables are ready!

$\mathcal{F}$OUR

Weight Has...

...always been an issue for me. For the better part of my youth, I was what you'd call a big girl. You know her. She's that girl whose face would always conjure up a compliment because you couldn't see all the way around the rotundness of her body to compliment anything else.

I never thought of myself as 'gigantic' because I was smaller than most of my friends. Now they were heifers! (Sorry girls, but you know who you are!) So yeah, weight has always been a big issue in my life. Now don't get me wrong, it's not that I'm grossly overweight in the physical sense, but my brain always tells me different. I think that makes me like most women who've had these little [or big] battles with their body identity when your weight is constantly fluctuating.

I suffer from what many middle-agers suffer from…that dastardly, annoying, freaking spare tire-ish bulge that seems to gather around our waist while we're not paying attention.

What come's to mind when I happen to catch a glimpse of this stockpile of flesh is elephant ankles, where the skin just seems to lay in layers. Part of this problem of course is due to menopause. My menopause! That wonderful part of a woman's life where she becomes at risk for injuring people around her, especially when your estrogen hits an all time low. At least that's what I tell myself.

Okay, I may bitch about menopause, but it does have some perks. We can lay blame to a lot of things that happen to our body and our mind during these non-blood-letting years. Thank God for small favors right?

Something I find kind of interesting is how belly fat has become big business. The main target for these ads we see on television or in magazines are women, especially the ones who've earned their baby badges. Every day you see those asinine ads for pills, patches, and smoothies that promise to reduce your protrusions with little or no effort. You know the ones. Pop a pill starting Monday and drop a few clothing sizes by Friday.

HELLOOOOOOOO...

Is anyone out there really buying this crap? Are we that stupid? I mean really!

Okay...so I've sent for a few of these products. Admittedly, I am one of those idiots! I got sucked in by a few of those smooth talking salespeople who made it sound so easy, so believable, *soooooo* promising.

I followed the plan, popped a pill, and waited. And then I waited some more, and a little more after that. Was my ass or gut shrinking? No! Not even one teensy-weensy inch. The *ONLY* thing that got smaller was my stinking bank account!

You might as well just find a drug dealer who can supply you with speed, or better yet, just drink espresso all day. All these pills did was make me talk faster and run around like a chicken with its head cut off. Another side affect from these 'oh so safe products' is the shaking. You know that nervous twittering you get when your blood sugar is too low or you've caffeine overloaded. Maybe this is how you actually lose the weight–you just bloody shake it off.

I'm not exactly sure what the ingredients are because I've never been into reading labels. What

I do know though, is that they drove my ADD into hyper-drive. This pissed my husband off, because on occasion (I've always been the 'handyman' of the house) I've been known to strip a room down to its studs in less than four hours rather than just splash a new coat of paint on the walls to get the same effect.

Oh yeah, those $30 miracle pills cost us about $40,000 to rebuild our kitchen one year.

So, working on the premise of 'been there, done that', I came to the conclusion that any extra pounds I've acquired, well, they're just going to have to come off the good old-fashioned way—starvation and exercise.

I knew I had to make a plan and so plan I did. Me and the hubby (whose idea of exercise is moving the fork from the plate to his mouth) started walking every morning. This is not only good for the body (fat) it's also a great way to clear your head. We'd try to get in at least a mile and a half each day. We'd been doing this faithfully for about a year, but then I fucked that up. I discovered a shortcut. We could finally do our mile in under half a mile! Duh!

Another brilliant realization I came to because I'm such a clean freak, was that I could use normal household appliances as part of my cardiovascular workout if you indeed believe the shaking theory.

I have this horrible bad habit of loading my

laundry machine in an uneven way. It used to piss me off listening to it bounce around trying to escape from its built in space, but then, the more I thought about it, the more I realized that maybe it was trying to tell me something. Maybe it had been trying to get my attention all along.

I stood there one morning watching as it gyrated to and fro and it occurred to me that there was a good possibility it could help in my endeavor to slim down. (Yes, we're back to the shaking theory.)

At first, I just leaned against it, kind of testing the waters you know. Oh boy! That was a real eye opener. All of a sudden I could feel my loose flesh slopping back and forth, kind of like those waves you see in a pool after someone does a cannonball.

I found this quite depressing because I realized there were things moving that I didn't expect to move. You know, things like my recently acquired double chin. Oh yeah. I know it's there. I've seen pictures. Hell, that's why I always hold my chin up so high now. Do you know how many reflective surfaces you come across in a day? They're everywhere!

Oh, and Thing One and Thing Two have let me know unequivocally that they don't like to entertain uninvited guests.

The other double chins, the ones that hang loosely on the underside of my upper arms were also having a hay-day. My butt…hell…that sucker was dancing the salsa.

So much for plan A!

I knew that I'd have to figure out a way so that I didn't actually feel this stuff, my fat, moving around as though it were possessed by the devil himself. After pondering on this for a day or so, plan B unfolded in a moment of brilliance.

Because I'm very conscious of my flaws I have several undergarments that forcefully mold these devilish curves back to where they're supposed to be. It was simple. I'd don one of these (priceless) one-piece thingies under my housecoat. Then I'd throw on a pair of running shoes and off to the laundry room I'd head. I'm usually doing the laundry in the middle of the night because I suffer from insomnia (thank you menopause) so it was very unlikely I would be found out. As a matter of fact, I don't think anyone in my house actually knows where the laundry machines are anyway.

Well, thank God my family is incredibly slobbish when it comes to their clothes because there's never a lack of laundry that needs to be tended to. I'd be able to do this every day.

Taking this experiment one step further I decided it was time to jump on board. I hoisted myself up on top of the 'NOW-ON-PURPOSE-OVERLOADED' machine and pushed the button. Whee hah! It was like riding one of those electric bulls at a country fair. I would not recommend drinking coffee while doing this unless you put it in one of those travel mugs. Oh well, more laundry for me.

Now, this is quite a tricky process because there's a good possibility that the machine will buck you off like a pissed bronco bull, so you've got to figure out how to brace yourself. The doorframe was a good start. I could put one foot up against it and then I moved the big cabinet that holds all my tools a little closer so there'd be a place for the other foot. It's not exactly a pretty sight but it seemed to do the job.

I figure I can get in about two hours of this before the sun comes up so there's no chance of getting busted in my ridiculous looking pose, wearing things no one should see publicly.

There's also another perk I must mention while using this method. Not only does the machine gyrate, it also vibrates if you get my drift. Yes, I go about this chore happily now. My children think I'm nuts because I'm always gathering up their clothes now–dirty or not. I'm not going to tell them any different.

The other thing I invested in are those rubbery ropes, the ones you do resistance exercises with. They've got little handgrips on either end so they're fairly easy to use. Using these started out with a bang, and then my decision to stop using them also came with a bang.

If you're going to work with them outside in order to work your back, you have to sling it over something to add resistance. Well, let me tell you if you choose a tree branch, it better be a big ass tree branch. I couldn't reach the big thick ones so I made the mistake of using a lower thinner branch, which did not pan out. It only took two pulls before the twiggy little bugger broke free and crashed into the bridge of my nose. It was at this point I realized these particular workout tools also make excellent garden tiebacks.

All in all, I'm getting it together this year. My New Year's resolutions have unfolded. I've vowed to walk slower. This way, things I don't want to move don't, or at least not enough to attract attention. And since we're still using the short cut for our walk, the slower pace makes it feel like we've actually walked the whole damned mile and a half again.

I've vowed to look in the mirror once in the morning while I'm getting ready and then avoid anything that might reflect my image during the rest of the day.

I've vowed never to give my fat and fatter clothes away again.

I've vowed to tell myself I'm not fat–I'm just not thin. You know... bullshit things. A girl's gotta do what a girls gotta do, right?

So there you have it in a nutshell. I'm starting this year off with a fresh start. I'm going to get in shape or at least shape what I got.

I'm going to try to regain some of that M.I.L.F. factor back. I know I've passed my prime point so I won't be hanging out anywhere near a middle or high school, although I've recently discovered a new senior living center near my house that is starting to look promising as far as gawkers go.

Maybe I'll start a new trend!

I'm going to become a S.I.L.F. (Senior I'd Like To Fondle)!

$\mathcal{F}$IVE

$\mathcal{E}$xercise $\mathcal{I}s$...

...sometimes like corporal punishment. We brutalize our poor little muscles mercilessly in hopes they'll shape up as fast as possible. We stress and strain them, often times beyond their capacity, and then wonder why they seek revenge the day after, or the day after that. They're smart little buggers. They can tie you up like a pretzel on crack.

Yes, they're sneaky little bastards!

— Jacqui Brown —

My last personal trainer's favorite phrase was, "Do twenty more".

I'd look at him with my best *'fuck you'* glare.

Twenty more and they'll be picking out a pine box for me.

Twenty more and I might be picking out a pine box for him.

"My fat does not want to do twenty more," I'd tell him.

He'd glance at my gut knowing this would hit home. I'd cuss him under my breath but start counting.

"One, two, three…"

Bastard!

By the twelfth curl, I'd feel that muscular flaming sensation building itself up to bonfire status.

"Why are we using such big weights," I'd ask while trying desperately to suck in a breath.

"They're only two pounds," he'd say.

"Oh," I'd say, turning the weight so I could make sure he wasn't bullshitting me!

The thing about trainers is that they've already done all the work they need to on themselves so they're well aware of the pain they're inflicting on you. Do they emote any sympathy towards you as you struggle through each exercise? Hell no! They just tell you to shut up and quit whining.

What I hated most about my trainer was, when I'd start moaning and grunting like a pig during our weight lifting sessions, he'd take his fingers and strum the fat on the underside of my upper arm like a virtuoso harp player just to make his point.

I'd try desperately to ignore his mockery of my fat flags and his snarky little grin. The whole time I'd be thinking, with very little effort, I could probably make contact with the side of his head with that little *'two-pound'* dumbbell clenched in my sweaty palm.

Oh yeah! I'd picture him slowly melting towards the ground shortly after impact, completely unconscious, in which time, I could pour water over my head and down the front of my shirt in order to mimic sweat. Then all I'd have to do is sit down next to him and wait. When he'd come to I'd simply wipe my brow then say, wow, that was a good workout. See you next week!

Unfortunately, I could never actually go through with it because we worked out at a public park. There would be witnesses. I had to force myself to stay in control and out of trouble.

Of course, by this time, he'd gotten that underarm fat moving so fast, it was actually creating a nice little breeze that kept me cool.

"…eighteen, nineteen, twenty."

At that point I'd feign exhaustion then let the weights drop from my hands in hopes that one of them would meet with his foot. But he was always too fast. He knew me too well. He'd step back, smile, and then bark out what was next.

"Squats," he'd say.

"How many?" I'd ask.

"Fifteen," he'd say.

I hate, hate, hate squats! I like what they do for my butt, and I like what they do for my legs, but I fucking hate doing them, but not for the reason you might be thinking. The word *'squat'* and the menopausal gastrointestinal system DO NOT go together.

Once that word left his lips, all I could think about was whether or not I'd taken my Gas X that morning.

He'd tap his watch and wait for me to spread my legs, square my shoulders, and then raise my arms out in front of my body hoping to keep some semblance of balance. I'd start to lower my body ever so slowly. One inch. Two inches. Three inches!

It's then I'd remember that I didn't take that little green pill. I'd meant to—I really did. I'd popped it out of its little vacuum-sealed package but then set it down on the kitchen counter while I went to retrieve a bottle of water. I never revisited the counter though.

Oh no!

I knew right away this was not going to be good. Somebody was going to get hurt here!

"Go deeper," he'd say.

I'd feel my stomach starting to gurgle. It wanted to purge itself in a big way.

"Now," he'd bark at me as he put his hands on my shoulders pushing me towards the failure position.

I'd close my eyes and put all my concentration on keeping my sphincter muscle clamped tight. Ladies, this is where all those Kegel exercises you learned during pregnancy come in handy.

I'd go down a few more inches as requested and as always, I'd feel my knees starting to shake. I could also feel one of those humongous gas bubbles traversing around in my gut like a slalom racer looking for the gate.

OMG!

I knew I could only do about two or three more of these dips before this situation reached the *'Houston, we've got a problem'* stage'. I knew my limit and so did my sphincter muscle!

"Two," he says out loud as though in my aged state I've lost my ability to count.

I'd suck in my lower belly as I rose hoping somehow to push this bloody gaseous troublemaker back up to where it started. No dice my body tells me. This puppies gonna blow pretty damn soon.

My mind would be racing by this time as I mentally searched for a way to make this stop. But then I start thinking, maybe it'd be one of those polite silent farts, and if there is a God, it wouldn't be one of those Chernobyl stinker's that are rotten enough to take out an entire neighborhood.

He'd move in closer to better control the depth of the squat, and all I could do was concentrate on keeping my butt cheeks together.

As you can imagine, this is nearly impossible in this position.

Then it would occur to me that this strategy would eliminate any possibility of silence.

If the gas left my butt during the tightening of the cheeks it would likely come out sounding like one of those canned air horns. I'd have to think on my feet and make some kind of decision. Let her rip and take my chances it would just blow out like a soft gentle breeze, or publicly acknowledge that I had a rip-roaring case of gas.

But wait. If I let Mother Nature take its course and let it blow in its full glory, the sound ringing out like a proud duck quacking with a cold, this might put an end to this particular exercise. Maybe he'd see that it was not in his best interest, or mine, to force my body into this ridiculous position.

Oops!

Too late! My bad!

Half way down on the second squat my body took control, my sphincter relaxed and justice was served. It was not polite, nor was it as quiet as I'd hoped it would be. As a matter of fact, a few people passing by us during this assault, actually looked up in the sky searching for the flock of ducks they'd just heard.

"Jesus Christ," he said looking down at his legs to make sure I hadn't left skid marks on his tight white workout pants.

"What?...What are you talking about?" I'd say pointing to the people looking up into the sky. "Didn't you see them, the ducks?"

He'd follow their gaze searching the clear blue sky for any sign of birds.

Then it would hit him.

The air surrounding us was so toxic it rippled the same way hot summer sun does over cool asphalt. It smelled so bad, the end of his nose actually curled in such a way as to close itself off from the foulness.

Distraction is the best defense so I began to squat one more time.

"Noooooo," he'd manage to squeak out while trying to hold his breath. "We're done with those."

Great, I tell him, then ask him what he wants to do next.

"Shower," he'd say.

"Oh, okay. I'll see you next week."

"No…I think I'm busy next week."

As I stood there digesting his comment I realized that we were done–forever–so I bent over to pick up my towel and delivered a parting prize.

I guess I should be grateful he dumped me. All the money I'd been spending on getting in shape has now been diverted to purchasing the big box of Gas X from Costco.

My entire family is extremely grateful to him for this very reason because, well, now I have to work out at home.

Six

Hormones Are...

(Part 1)

...to a women's body what motor oil is to a car. Let one or the other run dry, and you're gonna be stuck with a cracked block, spark plugs that don't fire, or worse yet, a completely fucked up, out of commission engine. This is not a good thing for you or anyone in close proximity.

Not only will your crankshaft be cranky, your

axle frozen—you'll also discover that your tranny and oil pan will no longer be willing to accept a dipstick!

Oh yes, these little hormone buggers are the nectar of life for women who've begun that descent into that 'middle place'.

In my book, anything is game when the well's run dry!

I knew something was really wrong when I started cursing at inanimate objects around the house.

My brand spanking new refrigerator was the first to suffer under my barrage of obscenities. It failed me so many times in my plight to ward off hot flashes. It's one of those new fancy-schmancy energy-efficient ones with all the compact shelves. Once you've shopped and piled the stuff inside, there's little or no room for any body parts. Not even my teeny-weeny head. The only appliance, as you very well know, the only one that is off-limits to my tirades is my darling washing machine. *We* have a *special* relationship.

So once again, I dragged my ass off to the doctor's office, rolled up my sleeve, stuck my arm out, and demanded they draw blood.

"I'm ready, go ahead," I said waving my arm in front of her.

The young tech approached warily.

Being around anyone who is hormonally imbalanced can strike absolute fear in even the most confident professional.

She motioned me towards the chair. I stomped over and plopped down in the worn leather seat.

"You're gonna feel a little prick," she said.

"I know, my husband already told me the same thing this morning," I shot back.

She blushed, but otherwise ignored my glare. She tied off my upper arm to create pressure, then used two very cold fingers to tap the area where my veins were supposed to be. After a few minutes of this she decided she's found a likely target and jabbed the needle into my flesh. She twisted the needle back and forth like she's excavating a fucking mine.

"Um, you're hurting me," I said.

"No I'm not, if you'd stop squirming," she replied.

"I'm not squirming. I'm sitting here like a rock," I said. "You're the one squirming."

"No...I'm not squirming, I'm just trying to find your vein," she spit back at me.

"It's right there...I can see it plain as day," I offered.

"No. That's not the right vein, it's not the one I need," she said.

"Don't you just need one with blood in it?" I ask.

"Shhhhhh…!" she said trying to ignore me.

"You're shushing me?"

"Yes," she said.

I could see her frustration level building, and I knew that this could go from bad to worse at any moment.

"Maybe you should try the other arm," I offered.

"Maybe you should just shut the hell up and let me do my job," she snapped back.

It's pretty hard not to notice, that after two or three minutes have passed, there has yet to be even one drop of blood drawn.

"Hmm….", I utter as I watch that little elbow crook starting to turn black and blue.

"I'm going to try the other arm," she says withdrawing the needle.

"Whatever!" I said.

We repeat the procedure, tie off the arm, pat the skin, stick the needle in, and start searching once again for the elusive vein.

I decide to concentrate on the lively conversation going on between two of the other nurses in the office. They just happen to be discussing gardening.

"It took all day to dig that sucker out," says nurse #1.

"I know what that's like. I had this tree once whose roots were everywhere. Took me the better part of the day to get them all out," nurse #2 replies.

"Hey...pssst...you there!" I say to get their attention. "You guys should hire this one, she can dig like nobodies business."

"Ouch," I said as she twisted the needle in revenge for my comment.

I see the smirk on her face.

BITCH!

"Sorry," she says, as though I'd actually believe her.

"Maybe someone else should do this," I say hoping she'll stop moving the fucking needle around.

"Why are you whining," she asks.

"I don't know. Maybe because you've been in there seven or eight minutes now and there's still no blood in that little vial," I respond with as much bitch in my voice as hers.

That does it for her. She pulled the needle out, undid the little rubber tourniquet, and ripped it away from my arm. Of course now all the hair that was under the little rubber thingy is now missing, but she doesn't seem to care.

"I'll get the doctor," she says smiling.

"WHAT? Shit!" I think to myself.

She spins on her heels and stomps away from me. I hear her shoes clickity-clacking all the way down to the end of the hall.

Then–dead silence!

The other nurses stare at me.

I love my gynecologist but she's one of those slam, bam, thank you ma'am kind of doctors. There's no fucking around with her. She's a specialist so her time is very valuable. She's that 'git er done' gal.

The spark of fear hits me when I hear *her* heels clomp-clomping on the pristine wood floors that she's recently installed.

I can feel my pulse begin to race. I know what I'm in for and I say to myself "Why can't you just shut your mouth you idiot. Now look what you've done!"

I can see from the look on her face she's not exactly happy to be called upon for this chore because I'm sure she has better things to do than try to suck my blood out.

"Hi there," I say hoping my friendliness will diffuse her ire because my veins are such a pain in the ass and she has far better things to do than this mundane simple procedure.

There is no response. Nada! Nothing! No eye contact. No *I'm sorry this is so difficult for you.* Not one peep. She just stares at the crook of my arm as she snaps the rubber gloves on. She grabs the little tourniquet and ties it around my other arm. As I look down to watch her in action, I'm fascinated by the fact that I can now see all the little hairs from my other arm waving around on the tourniquet as though they're saying goodbye because they didn't have time the first time round.

"How are the kids?" I ask trying to get her to relax a little.

"FINE," she says sounding really annoyed. Then I remembered! When you have kids, you're never relaxed, never fine. Wrong question I guess.

Bam!

Needles in and the exploration begins all over again.

I grit my teeth forcing my mouth to stay shut. I watch the needle zigzag North and South, then

East and West.

The whole time I'm wondering, where the fuck is my blood? Had it too gone the way of my hormones?

"I guess I'm just fresh out," I say jokingly.

Her expression turns to one of stern concentration. By now my toes are curling up inside my shoes, and it's hard to keep my ass down on the chair. Another twist, another turn and I'm now ready for take off. But then wait! I see one precious drop of blood slowly sliding down the side of the clear glass vial.

"Eureka," I yell out.

"We're *almost* there," she says.

She plunges the needle deeper and a little to the left then a little to the right, and suddenly, there it is. That wondrous red liquid is now flowing into the tube at a rapid rate.

"Fucking A Beatch!"

She looks up at me, and it's then I realize I said this out loud.

"Are you whining?" she asks.

Again, I deny that I'm whining as I blink back the tears I'm trying to force back into my tear ducts so she doesn't think I'm a complete pussy.

She rips the tourniquet off so the blood will flow like a river. Again, I notice there is now a new barren spot on this arm as well. I'd once considered shaving that unsightly hair off my arms and this might just be the catalyst for doing just that.

My body, after all this trauma, is more than willing to give up eight or so vials of blood.

I ask her if she needs more than that?

She shakes her head no!

I ask her if she can just keep some on file so we don't have to repeat this dastardly procedure for a while?

Again, that look, the one that tells you you're a complete moron, and could you please just shut the hell up.

"We'll call you with the results," she says sliding the needle out of my arm.

She rips the gloves off and without further ado, makes her way back down the hall to her 'real' patients.

I roll my sleeve down and go over to the desk to check out.

"That'll be $40 dollars," the receptionist says.

"$40 dollars? I'm gonna need that to buy makeup

to cover these marks on my arm," I tell her.

"Funny," she says. "Give me the $40 bucks."

"Whatever," I shoot back.

Three o'clock that afternoon the phone rings.

"I've got good news and bad news," the receptionist says.

"What's the good news," I ask her.

"Your check cleared," she says.

"What's the bad news," I ask.

"You've got no hormones," she says.

"None?" I ask.

"None, nada, nothing. You're running on empty," she says. "You need to come back right now and we'll give you some."

"Will there be any little pricks involved?" I ask, not knowing anything about the delivery of such medications.

"No, just cream," she says.

Again, I'd heard the same thing from my husband that same morning after the 'little prick thing' was denied. I was starting to feel like they were all conspiring against me.

"I'll be there in ten minutes," I tell her.

"We'll be waiting with bated breath," she says, as though mocking a women in my condition is not a bad thing.

Ten minutes later I open the door to their office. The nurses scatter trying to avoid direct contact with me now that I'm officially a walking time bomb.

"Should I come in?" I ask motioning to the door that leads to the examination rooms.

"Noooooooo!!!!!! Stay where you are," the receptionist manages to squeak out. "I'll show you what to do from here if you don't mind."

She shoves a small bottle across the counter. I pick it up and pop the top off. She does the same with her sample bottle.

The demonstration lasts about five seconds. Pump once, rub the cream on your forearm.

I do what I'm told, then I stand there waiting for some kind of reaction. All three nurses just stare at me wondering what I'm doing.

"WHAT?" I bark at them as their eyes widen in fear.

"Ummmm…it takes about two to three weeks to take effect," she says taking a few steps back from the counter.

"Excuse me?" I ask as though I've heard her wrong.

"Look, I'm just the messenger," she says. "It takes two to three weeks before you'll start feeling more like yourself."

"Whatever," I say.

I toss the bottle into my bag and as I turn to leave, I see a few of her pregnant patients sitting there, staring at me. They look somewhat frightened. I don't know if it's the look on my face that's making them fearful, or the realization that this is what they have to look forward to.

"Yeah, that's right. Enjoy your hormones while you've got em! Oh, and good luck with your vagina after you push that sucker out," I say directly to the tiniest woman with the biggest belly, then quickly leave the room slamming the door behind me. I don't think I got more than three steps away from the door when I heard the lock engage.

Hormones can make or break you in so many ways, it's hard not to laugh when the going gets tough. Although I've recently discovered that at my age, this kind of laughter can also significantly increase your chances of accidentally pissing down your own leg at the most inopportune time.

When hormones are raging, as in you actually still have some, it's likely the time when we're ready to hatch those little parasites...er...I mean those sweet little angels we call our children.

Oh yes, I remember those glory days when my skin was taut and flawless. Yes, I was full of elasticity then. My hair was shiny. Those ugly brown age spots had yet to surface, and I could usually bounce back from whatever came my way as far as my body went.

Now that I've surpassed that time, I only use the term elasticity when shopping for pants, as in "do these come with an elastic waistband?" or "how much give does this spandex shit really have?"

I no longer try not to acknowledge that bounce in my step, because I know that 'that bounce' is usually just my softer, rounder fat ass trying to stay contained in my trendy, hip, low-cut jeans.

After seeing my gynecologist, and trying out the estrogen gel, I knew things would eventually be okay. Even though these miracle hormones hadn't kicked in yet, I was by no means ready to throw in the towel.

Some say I've got the patience of a saint. These of course, are the same people who've never seen me behind closed doors.

Let's face it. If I had reality camera's rolling in our house 24/7, one of us, probably me, would likely be carted away to some nice, freshly painted, white walled facility by some kind of pepper-spray packing, uber-polite, uniformed professional.

SEVEN

Hormones...(Part 2)

(To Hair Or Not To Hair?)

After chewing on this hormone thing over the next few weeks, I decided to investigate my options. I'd heard so much about bio-identical hormones, I started asking all my girl friends if they'd ever tried it, and as it turns out, nearly all of them went bio-identical. I jumped on board and starting making some calls.

Turns out that there's not too many doctors who

specialize in it, probably because of our fucked up health insurance system. Those who do, are booked so far in advance, it takes months of waiting till you can go see them. But again, this is where my patience pays off. I book an appointment for...what the fuck...two months down the road. Oh Lordy. This was really going to be a test of my stamina and patience! It was also going to be an interesting time for my family.

As it turns out, my gynecologist is not big on these homeopathic solutions. She thinks they're a bunch of hoey-baloey because pharmaceutical hormones are, as she says, an exact science. But that did not deter me. I was not going to let her rain on my parade. Of course, now all I had to do was convince her to send my blood test results to this new gal so I wouldn't have to revisit that hideous blood drawing experience any time soon. Two arm-wrestles later–I won!

I'm glad I jumped on this right away because as it turns out, my body was not absorbing the gel like it should have. All the death glares I was shooting out like ray vision in a sci-fi movie, brought on by my estrogen depletion, should have been the first hint that something was amiss. I now, single-handedly, had the ability to empty a room in less than three seconds just by making my presence known.

Tick tock, tick tock!

Anticipating this consultation was nearly enough to kill me as I counted the weeks, days, hours, minutes, and seconds until I could walk into this appointment demanding to be fixed.

Being ever the resourceful woman I am however, I came up with the perfect solution to throw whatever was or was not happening in my body off-balance.

I discovered that the agave plant has medicinal qualities.

That's right–tequila.

Halle*fucking*lujah!

That last day before my appointment seemed to crawl along like a snail trying to maneuver up a greased hill. I paced. I sat. I read. I surfed the net till my fingertips were raw. As a matter of fact, I think I Googled every stinking word that popped into my head.

I kept looking at the clock hoping it would hit my bewitching hour, wherein I could at long last crawl into bed so I could stop all this waiting nonsense.

Anticipation really is a bitch too!

6:05.

6:17.

6:17 & ½.

This was not going well so I turned my attention

back to that agave.

By eight o'clock that night, that little worm at the bottom of the bottle and I were having a perfectly normal, reasonably superficial conversation.

"Swim you little bastard," I chanted.

"No, no senora, I am dead. I no can swim no more," he replied.

"Bastard," I said leaning in closer to the bottle trying to decide whether he was telling the truth or not.

I guess I should've read the warning label on the back of the bottle.

This product can produce hallucinatory side effects.

...as in one tequila, two tequila, three tequila, floor!

I think I met that quota sometime just before midnight, because I couldn't actually remember going to bed.

Finally, morning rolls around. It's '*the day*'! My head is pounding. My tongue seems to be sticking to the top of my mouth because I can't seem to produce any saliva. And, I have this weird recollection of speaking to the dead.

Regardless of my self-indulged hangover, I

shower, dress, jump in the car and head out to my appointment. It was going to take me about forty minutes to get there so I'd given myself plenty of time without having to rush like a mad woman. Morning traffic in Los Angeles is God's way of punishing us for waking up and thinking it's going to be a good day.

Surprisingly enough though, there's hardly any traffic at all and I get there in record time. This is not something that happens that often in our wondrous city and I feel grateful for this little favor.

"Good morning," I say as perkily as I can, obviously trying to hide the fact that I'm incredibly hung over. "I'm Jacqui. I'm here to see the doctor."

"Just have a seat, she'll be with you shortly," she said.

"Is she running on time?" I query.

"Um…she's actually not here yet," she replied.

"WHAT?"

"You're forty-five minutes early," she says pointing to the clock.

I look at her clock and then at my watch.

Crap! Then it dawns on me. That's why I got such a good parking spot.

Tick-tock, tick-tock.

I read through every magazine in the waiting room as my ADD kicked in.

Finally, the door next to the receptionist opens and I hear them call my name. I don't know why she had to say my name out loud. I was the only one in there. A simple nod would have done the same trick.

I step through this magical portal expecting to feel some sort of transformation, some form of relief, but nothing happens.

Anyway, I follow her down the hall to a teeny-weeny room. She tells me to sit down. Tells me the doctor will be right in. Tells me to relax.

Hell, if I wanted to relax I'd just go buy myself another 'worm' swimming pool!

Tick-tock, tick-tock!

To me, homeopathy is sort of like the twilight zone. You're not exactly sure what to believe, but you're so willing to go there because it just sounds so grown up, so healthy and so smart.

So there I am waiting some more. I survey the room and wonder where the ethereal music is? I wonder why there's no spa like feeling coursing through my brain (or the room)? Why was there no smell of pleasing aromatherapy oil? Where were the healing crystals I expected to see? Where was that magical aura I was expecting?

Where the fuck was the doctor?

My ADD kicked into full blast and my anxiety started to rear its ugly head so, rather than just sit there letting my mind get the best of me, I rearranged the furniture and all the art on the walls.

Ten minutes later, in walks this blonde bombshell. She stops just inside the door and surveys the room then looks at me. I know she's thinking she might have gone into the wrong room. That she's mistakenly walked into the psychotherapist's appointment by mistake. She checks the number on the door and then looks directly at me.

"Are you Jacqui?" she asks.

"That would be me!" I say.

"Okay. Nice job on the room by the way!" she says returning her gaze to my file. I think she's already sensing that there could be trouble.

The white coat hugging her youthful curves tells me she must be the doctor. I'm still awed by the fact that she looks like a fucking movie star. All I can think about now is that, I should have taken more time to do my hair and makeup.

I try to sit up straighter but remnants of my self-induced hangover keep me slumped over like a dog out of treats.

"Good morning," she says with enough perk in her voice to command global peace.

"Grrrrrrr...." is the only response that leaves my lips.

I'm wondering why she's so happy and why she's talking so loud, but then I realize again, it's only because of my overindulgence of the agave juice that everything seems out of proportion.

She leafs through the paperwork I've filled out, and then scans my blood test results.

"OH MY..." she says taking a step or two back.

"Can you fix me," I ask.

"Absolutely," she says.

A slew of questions later, she explains how she's going to treat me.

"We're going to give you estrogen," she says then writes something in my file. "How's your sex life?"

"My sex life?" I ask.

"Yeah, how's your sex life?" she asks once again.

"What sex life?" I respond.

"You know...the one where you have sex," she says.

"Oh, that sex life…mmmmm….!" I say needing to think this through for a minute. "It's, you know…"

"How's your libido, your sex drive, do you want to have sex?" she asks.

Now I'm a little stunned by her question because I see she's wearing a wedding ring, and gay marriage is still illegal in California.

"Are you asking me if I want to have sex with you," I respond. I'm a little shocked by her brevity. Even with my hangover I wasn't expecting her to be so forward.

"No, not with me, with your husband!" she says.

"Oh," I say feeling a little rush of embarrassment course through my body. I'm surprised she didn't add 'you idiot' to the end of her sentence.

"Libido's not too good," I tell her. "Can you fix that too?"

"Of course I can," she says writing a note in my file. "You need testosterone."

She begins to explain how this chemical works in the female body, and I'm thinking, hell yes, I'm totally game for this.

"There's a few side affects you should know about though," she says.

"Side affects? Like what?" I ask.

"Well…you might grow a few stray hairs here and there," she says.

"Stray hairs?" I ask.

"Yeah, like maybe on your face. Sometimes other places too!" she tells me like it's no big deal.

My hand impulsively shoots up to my face. My fingers start rubbing that spot under my chin where I'm constantly plucking out a couple of very coarse, very dark stray eyebrow hairs.

"How many stray hairs are we talking about?" I ask.

"Maybe just a few, sometimes a lot," she says.

I have this sudden urge to pull open my shirt so I can see my boob, the one that loves to cohabitate with a tiny group of strays. I try to picture my nipple wearing a toupee and this disturbs me.

"Are we talking shaving or plucking hair amounts?" I query.

"There's a possibility of both," she says.

"Oh," I say.

As she starts reading my file again, I reach into my purse and find my glasses so I can see her better. This is when I notice several incredibly long hairs dancing around under her chin. I lean in to get a better look and see several more wisps on her cheeks. I realize, by the looks of things, she's a natural blonde.

"Do you take testosterone?" I ask.

"Yes I do," she says still perusing my file. "My husband said he doesn't care if I start looking like Wolfman Jack, just so long as I want to have sex."

"Ohhhh…!" I say.

As though she can feel my eyes burning into her skin, she turns and looks at me.

"Why do you ask?" she says.

"Umm…no reason, just wondering," I answer trying to divert my attention away from the imaginary neon arrow I see pointing to these outgrowths on her face.

"Will it make me…you know…horny?" I ask.

"It should if the dosage is right," she says. "A lot of clients say that it works for them, but…"

"But what?" I ask.

"They say that they want to do everyone but their husband," she says smiling.

Interesting! I hadn't looked at men as eye candy in a very long time. Over the years, as my libido dribbled down my leg, they'd all sort of started looking more like unnecessary calories.

"I'll prescribe both," she says. "You should get them in three or four days. They come from a lab in Phoenix."

GREAT! HERE WE GO AGAIN—MORE WAITING FOR MOI!

Oh well, everything in its time I guess.

EIGHT

Hormones...(Part 3)

(Still Waiting)

Waiting is not my thing. It never has been. I want what I want when I want it, and that's that!

Tick tock, tick tock.

For three days I paced back and forth watching for the mailman. I felt more like a stalker than a woman waiting for her pesky bills to arrive.

On day four, I see him approaching my mailbox with a small package. Finally!

I run to the end of the driveway at break neck speed and stick my arm through the iron gate so he can bypass the box and put it directly in my hands. I'm sure I must look like one of those movie orphans begging for 'more please', but I don't care what he thinks as he watches my arm wave around like it's possessed, like I'm having some kind of epileptic seizure or something. Whatever is in that box is going to change my life, so leaving a good impression on him at that moment, is absolutely the last thing on my mind.

He hands me the mail and then hightails it back to his truck, but now his free hand is wrapped around his little spray can of pepper spray.

As I walked back towards the front door of my house, it felt like I was walking on cloud nine. It was like I was holding in my hands—the secret to life. The serum of youth. The magic that would turn me from mamma bear back into the cougar I once was.

My imagination during those magical moments of possibilities was running amuck because it felt like my skin was tightening with each step. Even better—I think I even felt a tingle in my groin. Oh, this was going to be good!

So that got me to thinking that, if just looking at the box was doing this, the actual taking of these precious little drops was going to be over the top.

I set the box down on the counter in my kitchen and got a knife from the drawer. With the precision of a sushi chef preparing a piece of fine tuna, I sliced the tape open, cracked open the top of the box, and there they were. Two little brown bottles filled with, well, I didn't exactly know what was inside them but I didn't care. The blonde bombshell doctor said this was going to solve a lot of the problems I was experiencing.

I took the bottles to my bathroom upstairs and shut the door. I wanted privacy because this felt like a right-of-passage to me. I was about to experience something that would turn back the hands of time. Something that would turn me into a sexual tigress. Something that would make me want to rip my own damn clothes off—or at least—that's what I was hoping for!

I opened the estrogen first and watched as the whitish serum uploaded into the little squirter thing. My thinking here was that, if I felt happier, horny would be achieved in no time.

I stuck my tongue up and out and raised the dropper towards my open mouth. I stepped closer to the mirror so I could see better and not miss the target.

One drop, two drops…

I swished them around in my mouth for about thirty seconds like directed, and then swallowed. Then, like an idiot, I stood there staring at myself as though I was actually going to witness something miraculous happening. I leaned in even closer to inspect the small nasty jowls that had changed my once lovely oval face into a some kind of boxy cartoon character shape, but nothing was happening. My dimples did not suddenly reappear as expected. My wrinkles remain untouched. And my neck…well, that little motherfucker of amassed freckled flesh, sat in the same puddle as before.

WHAT THE?

WHERE. WAS. THE. MAGIC?

My mind, as usual, reeled out of control at the thought that the other hormone, testosterone, was going to yield the same effect. But I persevered and uncapped it anyway.

One drop was all I was supposed to take but two fell into my mouth so fast it took me by surprise.

"Oops!"

My mind once again started racing forward.

Maybe I should have pre-lingeried in case I had a sudden urge to mount my husband.

I looked at my watch and again I waited.

There was one brief moment when I thought I felt my nipples tingle, but upon further inspection, it turned out to be nothing more than a few errant crumbs from my earlier breakfast toast rubbing relentlessly between the material of my bra and my skin every time I moved.

The anticipation of my clitoris turning into a heat-seeking vessel made my body flush for about one second and then nothing, nothing, and nothing!

What the...?

I bowed my head and started to pray that I could simply will this shit to kick in...but still nothing!

That's when I saw the tiny note at the bottom of the box. I picked it up and read it. A tear came to my eye.

It would take a few weeks for this stuff to kick in as well.

CRAP!

The first week passed slowly. Still nothing. No youth! No horny...Nada!

The second week brought a slight change. I was actually sleeping a little better than I had been so that was at least a little something.

I guess my husband had also been anticipating my sexual transformation as well because he was constantly walking around with a boner 'just in case' it kicked in.

That would also explain the pained look I kept seeing on his face whenever we were in the same room. He'd look my way and raise his eyebrows in question. He'd always look so hopeful, poor bastard! I'd look at him and shake my head 'no'.

It made me feel bad sometimes as I watched him saunter away like a deprived child; like a kid who'd been taken into a candy store but instructed not to touch anything.

This of course would also explain the new bottle of personal lubricant I discovered by his side of the bed. Poor bugger! If this shit didn't kick in soon, that poor man's arm was soon going to look like Popeye's arm. Or worse, I'd have to buy him one of those carpel tunnel wrist braces.

Somewhere during the middle of that second week though I noticed something really peculiar, nothing to do with my horny, just something odd.

I was blow-drying my hair early one morning, which was not anything out of the ordinary, but I had to keep stopping so I could figure out where the hell this foul odor was suddenly coming from. It was an assault as deadly as someone smacking me in the nose with a baseball bat. Every time I raised my arms it filled the room. I kept turning around to see if hubby had sneaked in, obviously checking for any progress, but to my dismay, I was the only one in the room.

I have not worn deodorant since I was in my teens because I never had to. I was blessed with sweet smelling sweat glands I guess. But this!!!! Whew!!!!! This was not good.

The blonde bombshell had forewarned me this could happen and so it was. I now smelled like an old truck driver who'd been on the road too long with no opportunity to shower.

I thought to myself, okay, wearing deodorant isn't that bad. I could do that no problem. It was no big deal.

But as suddenly as that thought came and went, I felt one of those hot flash panic moments take over my entire body.

Oh no!

If this was happening...

It occurred to me that I should look for the other foretold side affects as well. I set the blow dryer down and stepped closer to the mirror.

Holy crap! Those two little plucker hairs I'd finally made peace with beneath my chin had multiplied tenfold. That prompted me to open my housecoat and check out my one or two little nipple hairs.

Oh My God!

There was enough hair there now to actually do a little comb-over. Again I felt my body flush and started tearing through the drawer looking for my husband's shaver. No matter what else I'd let slide as far as my body was concerned, this was not going to be one of them.

By this time however, I could hear hubby coming down the hall towards the bathroom and I started to panic. I slid the shaver across my nipple and dislodged the little toupee in record time. I dropped the razor into the sink and threw a towel over it as the door opened.

In he walks with his morning boner. He sees me standing there with my housecoat open, my breast exposed, and his eyebrows shoot up in question. I know what he's thinking and it pains me horribly as I frown and shake my head in that 'no-fucking-way' motion once again.

His shoulders slump, as does his penis, and he heads towards the toilet.

Flash forward to month two.

TESTOSTERONE IS NOT MY FRIEND.

Body odor, hair shooting out of places it shouldn't were just not my cup of tea. The fact that I never got that 'fuck-me-now-or-die' feeling, and the fact that I was shaving more than my husband put a kibosh on the whole thing.

What really sealed the deal is when a friend of mine accidentally sent me a magazine story that was supposed to go to her boyfriend. It was titled, *What Your Facial Hair Says About You.*

Accident my ASS Bitch!

All in all, our sex life after thirty-three years is

still pretty damn great so why mess with it if it ain't *really* broken.

The estrogen on the other hand has made life more doable and more enjoyable.

I guess what it boils down to is you've got to pick your poison wisely. You have to learn to settle on being happy for even the smallest of wonders. You have to accept the fact that your vagina is now partially retired and is only willing to work part time.

Ah...Menopause!

$\mathcal{N}$INE

Meditation, Schmeditation...

...blah,blah, blah, blah, blah.

I have A.D.D!

You know, Attention Deficit Disorder!

This is not something my brain wants to wrap around—ever! Now don't get me wrong here. I would love nothing more than to stop my wandering mind from running like a racecar without a kill switch.

Unfortunately, it seems my mind has a mind of its own.

I've tried all the tricks.

I've tried burning candles so I could concentrate on the flame, but that didn't work out. From everything I've read, you're supposed to meditate in a very quiet place. In my house—there is no such place. The only room I could think of that might even remotely offer some semblance of solitude was my closet. All I had to do was clean a little space on the floor so I'd have room to sit and get a little table I could set a candle on, and voila—instant meditation quarters. Everything was going pretty good until I let out a big deep sigh as I was instructed to by the voice on the tape so I would feel more relaxed. Idiot! I'd forgotten just how little oxygen it takes to grow a flame. The tiny little wick exploded like a firecracker. I jumped up knocking it over and...well...after the nice firemen left, I realized I had made another bonehead choice.

It's safe to say that all I got out of that experience was more panic and a big bill for all the clothes I had to replace.

I've listen to a lot of those soothing, mind altering tapes, but always found myself dissecting and pooh-poohing the things they were trying to set deep into my brain. I guess deep down that makes me a sub-conscientious objector.

Nope. My brain has a separate motor that wants to waste all of its gas, all of the time.

I even tried yoga once or twice, but had to quit after my health insurance company denied my last claim. Unfortunately, the yoga instructor had to call the paramedics to rescue me. One thing you should know about me. When I do something, I do it with as much gusto as possible. Somehow, I'd gotten myself so tied up in a pretzel like position, they had to use the Jaws Of Life to get my legs untwined from around my neck. Who knew you could strangle your own damn self in the pursuit of peace and happiness?

DOG FACE DOWN–MY ASS!

I guess because I'm a writer, my brain is programmed to think at all times, day or night, come rain or come shine, come hell or high water. The shut off valve has either been hidden from me, or more likely, installed at birth by Toyota.

'Focus' is definitely not my strong point!

I'll start out the day like any other ordinary person. Usually laundry's the first order of the day. I can do this without waking any one up because my laundry room is outside, attached to my garage. I mean, what the hell else are you supposed to do at two or three in the morning when your brain refuses to lock down on the one thing you really want to do–write? I know I should do my exercises *every* time I'm out there, but the simple fact is, sometimes I have deadlines that need to be met.

Again, thank-you mid-life menopausal insomnia!

I'd put the dirty clothes into the machine, throw in some detergent and then, just as the lid shut, I happened to notice there's a chip in the paint on the wall behind the dryer. Before you know it, I'll have opened a can of paint, rustled through the cabinet where I keep my brushes, only to realize that I should clean out that cabinet so I can find things easier.

But that's when I notice an errant pack of seeds for marigolds and realize that Spring is just around the corner and these seeds should be in the ground by now. I don't have much of a green thumb (because my mother selfishly kept the green gene to herself) but every year I give it a shot.

When I go looking for my little shovel so I can plant these little treasures, I see a bush that needs to be trimmed and head off to the last place I think I left the shears.

I catch sight of my car and realize how dirty it is, and quickly go over to where the hose is so I can at least give it a quick rinse.

That's when I notice a few weeds that have popped up by the hose bib. Of course, that's when I remember that it's been leaking since the last time I used the damn hose. Some things just slip my mind as it races about randomly. In a matter of milliseconds, my last water and power bill flashes before my eyes, and I realize, this is why it was so damned high the prior month.

SHEESH!

I return to the cabinet to get a wrench, but then I notice that the trashcan is full and tomorrow's garbage day. I take the can down to the end of my driveway and dump it in the bin.

That's when I notice that the numbers, so carefully painted on the bins to keep my neighbors from 'borrowing' them, have faded to the point where they are unreadable so once again, I return to the laundry room to get the paint and stencil that will return them to their glory. I can hear that the washing machine is finished. I switch that load over, stuff the washer full of more dirty things, then I grab the paint stuff I need and actually, *miraculously*, make it all the way back to the garbage bins with no distraction. This almost never happens. I almost want to get down on my knees and thank God for this brief moment of focus, of clarity, of tunnel vision. But I don't because at that eye level, something else is bound to catch my attention.

By this time, the people who walk by my house early every morning, are starting to drift by. Some wave, some say *Hello*, and a few rudely ignore anything that resembles contact. Of course, if you're not used to what I look like that early in the morning it can be a pretty frightening sight.

Anyway, I set the paint down on the ground and attach the stencil to the front of the bin. That's when I see my next-door neighbor out walking her itsy-bitsy dog. I walk over to the fence and we chat for a while, and it's then I remember I still have to fix a hole in the fence where her dog somehow manages to squeeze itself through onto my property much to the delight of my Golden Retriever. He's wanted that bitch ever since she moved into the neighborhood. *MEN!*

I return to the cabinet once again and get some ties so I can reattach the extra fencing I've put in place to prevent this from happening, when just by chance I notice that one of my vines has come loose from the trellis along the walkway. I stop and take one of the ties and fix the problem. As I admire my work, I remember that there's a broken sprinkler head right behind the vine and I stoop over to see if the gardener has fixed it like I'd asked him to. Son of a bitch! It's still uncapped.

Back to the cabinet I head one more time because I can fix the bloody sprinkler head myself. When I reach in to get the little bag of fix it parts, the back of my hand grazes across something very sharp. That little light bulb goes off in my head because I realize this is where the tree trimming saw has been hiding all along.

I set the bag of sprinkler stuff on the washing machine for a moment, and dig the saw out because I'd been meaning to cut this bothersome branch off the tree in front of my office window for a while now. It ruins my view and needs to go immediately.

On the way back to the front of the house my toe catches the corner of one of the pavers on the path. Ouch! This will need to be fixed immediately. Last thing I need is for someone to trip over that and sue the shit out of me! I kneel down and start to pry the stone out of its little resting place. I realize I'm gonna need something to pry the stone up with, a mallet to hammer it back into place, and a little sand to finish the job. I set the saw down to one side and make the trip to the other side of the house where I keep all the big ugly stuff hidden behind a wooden fence.

The only way to get to this place is to go through the back yard. That's when I notice there's a few more errant weeds popping up around the fire pit. Fucking gardener! What the hell does he actually do when he comes here anyway? Now I'm going to have to spray these myself because the roots are buried deep down amid the rocks surrounding this gathering spot. Some kind of radar thingy clicks on inside my brain as it runs through my mental files searching through possible storage spots for the weed killer. I hide this stuff pretty well because I don't want the kids or the dog messing with it. A few seconds later, I get a brain flash and remember that it's upstairs on the top shelf of the closet in my bathroom. Of course, I also realize that this spot no longer makes sense because my youngest child is now six-foot-five and the dog is only interested in things he can chew that are crunchy! I sneak back into the house and move through the dark rooms like a stealth fighter so no one will be the wiser as to my whereabouts.

Before I get to the front stairs, I realize the dog has blocked my way. Even in the dark I can see him looking at me like "where's my Goddamned breakfast?" I return to the kitchen to feed him because if I don't, he'll start moaning and groaning, which means he may wake someone up. This is my alone time so I cannot, under any circumstances, allow this to happen.

I rip open the little packet of tasty, meaty morsels he's so fond of. I dump them into his soft food bowl, fill his other one with the stupid little hard bits he drags all over the damn house, and pour a bottle of mountain spring water into his water bowl. Again, he stands there looking at me like— is that it—one lousy packet? I've spent all night guarding your sorry asses and you give me one stinking packet of food? Jeez lady! What kind of joint are you running here?

Crazy thing is, I can actually hear these words in my head as I look him in the eye! Hmm! These short early morning conversations with my dog often leaves me wondering who's crazier, me or the evil eyed talking dog?

I catch sight of a cookie sheet the kids left out on the counter and move to put it away. But then, I vaguely remember promising them I'd make some cookies today—oatmeal—no cranberries, if I remember correctly. No time like the present I say to myself—out loud—louder than I'd planned!

CRAP!

Please God, let sleeping dogs lie! I stand there and listen for a moment but don't here a sound. Phew! Everyone is still sleeping.

I go to the cupboard to get the cookie mix out. Yes, you heard correctly! C-o-o-k-i-e M-i-x! (Not once in this book will you ever see the Martha Stewart side of me because it doesn't exist). I open the cupboard where I keep the mixing bowls and that's when I realize it's not in the cupboard. First I'm going to have to empty the dishwasher in order to get to the mixing bowl. I don't know what it is about dishwashers. I love to load it, but I absolutely hate the unloading part. I guess it must be that, when you put the dirty dishes in there's an anticipation thing. Once they're clean though, the thrill is gone! It's like looking at already opened Christmas presents.

I persevere. I put everything away, and that's when I see all the crap the kids left on the table after staying up too late. I set the mixing bowl down for a second and go to retrieve their dirty dishes.

I notice that there's a pile of crumbs on the floor that need to be cleaned up before the dog gets wind of them. I return to the kitchen to get the broom since it's too early to turn on the vacuum. I sweep the crumbs into a little pile and decide to finish the job and sweep the whole room.

When I go to dump the crumbs in the trash can I notice something has spilled down the front of the cabinet. I run some warm water on the sponge and scrub the little spot away. As I stand back to inspect my work, I notice that the light bulb above the sink is out. I go back out side to get the little stepladder because it's the only way to reach the burnt out bulb.

That's when I see the tree trimmer laying next to the path and get mad as I wonder who left the damn thing there. They knew I'd been searching for it.

As I bend to pick it up, I am suddenly attacked by a small white fluffy dog, and I hear my neighbor screaming for her precious AWOL pet. I remember immediately that I have not fixed the hole in the fence yet. I round up the puppy and hand her back over the fence when all of a sudden the bloody sprinklers turn on and I see a fountain like stream of water spewing out of the broken sprinkler, which neither I nor the asshole gardener has managed to fix yet.

I rush back to the laundry room to get the new sprinkler head, when suddenly the alarm on the dryer goes off and I remember it's time to change the laundry over one more time. I get the dry stuff out, stuff the wet clothes from the washer in, and then take the dry clothes inside so I can fold them.

That's when I hear my daughters alarm clock beep beeping and I realize, OMG, it's 6 a.m. I need to get her up so she won't be late for school. I do my morning ritual of screaming at her so she won't be late, pack, her lunch, then go outside to start her car so it's warmed up and ready to go.

That's when I notice how dirty my car is and………

Ten

Suppleness Is...

...a major concern for women of every age. Many of us who've passed the hormone marker, as in—we don't have any more, are constantly searching for the perfect combination of serum's that will lift, soften, and moisturize our skin.

We're constantly in pursuit of these miracle fluids or creams that can reduce those wretched wrinkles we lovingly refer to as smile lines that form around our eyes. We want something that will rid us of those hideous brown spots that seem to manifest themselves over night. We want something that will reduce the swelling and dark circles that appear underneath our eyes while we're sleeping. You know the ones I'm talking about–the ones that make it seem as though you've recently been involved in some sort of brawl. We want something that will eliminate those spidery veins that leave parts of our body looking like road maps.

We want, we want, we want!

It's an endless quest. It's expensive, and it's time consuming trying to track down these products that promise the fountain of youth, but we do it anyway.

No big deal right?

Vanity knows no boundaries I guess.

But here's my new dilemma.

Because I'm a major insomniac I watch television in the middle of the night when my writer's mind experiences what is known as writer's block. You can pretty much be guaranteed that most of what's on during these early morning hours are infomercials.

What's amazing and particularly cool about that is that it makes me realize I'm not alone. I'm not the only woman who rises at these ungodly hours because most of these adverts pertain to women's problem. There's apparently a big audience for them.

I've witnessed women losing 20 pounds of belly fat in ten days. Women growing a full head of hair back in less than a month. Women losing weight by popping a pill a day without having to change their diet. Women getting a face lift in under ten minutes. And oh my fucking God, women getting their ass-hole bleached for some God awful reason. I didn't realize this was a real thing you could do. I'd recently heard one of the old broads at my gym talking about it but I thought she was talking about her husband dying his hair. I remember the conversation so well because I'd only recently met her hubby and I was thinking to myself *he wouldn't look good blonde.* My bad! Guess I should have paid closer attention to the conversation.

The exercise infomercials that really irk me are those freaking cardio routine ones. You know the ones. You can't keep up, you trip over your own feet, and you have to take a five-minute break between every rep because your lungs no longer have the capacity to suck air in at that kind of speed.

What's really a pisser is that usually there's not one single female in the video who needs to lose one single stinking pound. Most of these bitches...I mean beautiful girls...are between the ages of eighteen and twenty-five. They already have protruding rib cages, and that perfect little line that runs down their perfectly concave belly defining their tight little abs. Their hair remains perfectly in place. Their makeup does not run. Their perfect teeth glow like neon Chiclets as their highly glossed, surgically altered, gargantuan pink lips part in smile. Their breasts, which are usually bursting out the top of their little skin-tight half-shirts, remain perky and immovable, and not one single ass cheek bounces around.

Never ever do they show some fat-ass woman wearing baggy ass clothes, sweating her fat ass off while gasping for air as they try to keep up the pace.

What the hell is up with that?

WHERE IS THE REALITY HERE?

Okay, so I have to admit that once in a while I'll bite the bullet and work out with them to make the time pass quicker. I'll grab my surviving resistance ropes, or my little weights, and follow along. I'll work hard enough to get to the burn they talk about, and I'll continue until the fail point, but then I stop. Why? Because my heart is sending out that message 'you stop or I'll stop'. When I get to this point, all I want to do is bitch slap the smile off their faces.

Oh yeah, I've been sucked in many times. I've picked up the phone within that golden 'ten minute time limit' to get the deal on their program, or pill, or cookie, or whatever they're hawking. I now own more exercise equipment than most gyms, most of which can be found hidden away in my 17 year-old man-child's room, or cave, as he likes to call it. He loves that I like these infomercials. He looks great! Me...not so much!

Yes, I am constantly being barraged in the middle of the night with a plethora of images and information on how I should be taking care of my body.

With so many things already to worry about in order to have a somewhat reasonable appearance, the last thing I ever thought I'd have to worry about is VD.

Yes, you heard me right–VAGINAL DRYNESS.

At my age, I'm apparently supposed to be worried about this. From what I understand now, almost forty percent of women my age suffer from this affliction.

'That's just fucking great,' I'm thinking to myself as I watch this stupid commercial that's somehow slipped under the FCC's critical eye. Like I don't have other things to worry about, now I have to worry about that little sucker too!

WHAT A BITCH!

So there I am at three in the morning wondering whether or not my vagina is worn out after fifty some years of workin' it.

Has it gone the way of my face?

OMG! Say it isn't so!

The thought of wrinkles and whatnot down there sends a shiver right through me. Should I go get this stuff and moisturize just in case, or should I just let sleeping dogs lie?

If you think about it, I mean really, a vagina get's put through its paces over the years.

A good night of sex is like sending your vagina to the gym. Sometimes the workout's slow and steady. Sometimes it's fat- burning cardio speed. Either way, I've always considered this a good thing.

Aside from the good exercise as stated above, our poor old vaginas have to endure years of menstruation, which is both a blessing and a curse. Then, when we decide to have babies, we pray that it'll play along when it's time to give birth because it's got to stretch and contort itself far beyond what it signed on for as that little pink bundle slides out into the world. That's a work out like no other, and all we can do afterwards is get down on our knee's and pray that it'll use common sense and somehow return to its normal size.

Seeing this commercial brought to mind a question my daughter asked me several years ago.

"Have you ever queef'd during sex?"

That was the first time I'd ever heard that word.

"Of course I have", I replied without blinking an eye.

My assumption was that it was when some sort of epiphany happened during sex.

She laughed her ass off at my response then went back to her room. Five minutes later she was still laughing. At that point I hightailed it into my office to look it up in the dictionary.

"Queef: (verb)…a vaginal fart during coitus.

No wonder she laughed. I'd definitely experienced that once or twice (okay, several times), but I'd never given it a name.

All this time I'd thought it was just my Ms. Vagina trying to catch her breath. My bad!

I digress.

Maybe those 'queef's' were a sign of some sort. Maybe that's the signal that you're headed towards a vagina that will soon be reminiscent of the Sahara Desert. One that is awaiting the presentation of an oasis in the form of vaginal moisturizer.

Based on its location, it's not easily accessible to your own eyes. The thought of asking the hubby about what he sees down there is completely out of the question. This is in line with 'if you don't draw attention to a problem people won't notice it'.

I think this is a gimme here!

I guess I have to decide which way to go here. Should I work under the premise that KNOWLEDGE IS POWER or IGNORANCE IS BLISS?

For now, I think I'll just forget that I ever saw that damned infomercial and simply assume Ms. Vagina still has the capacity to produce enough moisture to get me through another day, week, month, or if I'm lucky, another year!

*E*LEVEN

*H*ot *Sex*...

...is something we all strive for. Who on earth wouldn't? There's absolutely nothing else like being immersed in someone else's skin.

You know what I'm talking about. First you flirt, or ogle, if that's your style. Then you feel that little tingle start somewhere deep inside. Your toes start to curl up, and then suddenly your body is on fire. You're entire being is pulsating like a giant time bomb. The anticipation of a good orgasm keeps you in the moment. You start the countdown 10, 9, 8...

You're just about there when all of a sudden your mind wanders and you wonder whether or not you switched the laundry from the washer to the dryer…

CRAP!

Hot sex to me is when I accidentally burn my finger cooking dinner and I start hopping around the kitchen screaming 'fuck me, fuck me' while I dash to the sink to run cold water over it.

Of course this could actually lead to hot sex! If hubby's in the house, and he hears this gut wrenching scream, the next thing you know he's sprinting through the house at break neck speed to get to me. I've actually seen him break a sweat after maneuvering around the furniture in the living room, running hurdle over the dining room chairs, where upon entering the kitchen, he's already got his pants undone, and yep, there it is, the boner. Unfortunately, there's just some fuck me's that cannot be resolved with anything except cold water. This includes his boner.

Now don't get me wrong here. I am uber-grateful that after more than thirty-some years of marriage he still wants to jump my bones! He's forever grabbing my ass at the most unpredictable times and, while this is all well and good, I often wonder whether this is a sex thing or, is he just checking to see if I've been working out or not.

Sometimes he'll rub my shoulders only to let his hand wander down the front of my shirt.

Sometimes I stop him and sometimes I don't. It all depends on whether or not those little stray nipple hairs have been removed or not. It is not cool to have more hair on your chest than your husband. But all in all–it's all good!

Yes, in my world, hot sex is something that happens when the air conditioner isn't working. Oh there's plenty of steam and sweat, but I can't actually say it's caused by body movement.

There have been times when we're engaged in 'you know' and I get caught up listening to my spine cracking every time I move. Yes, at my age, it seems like all my bones are a little cranky when put to the test. My hip bones doth protest on occasion too and I wonder if I'll be stuck in that god-awful position forever. I do not want to walk around looking like I just got off a bronco bull.

I got an e-mail in my in-box the other day. You know the kind, the spam kind. The ones that randomly show up and pique your curiosity, especially the ones with the word *penis* in it. Well I clicked on the link and low and behold I got schooled on how long a man can have an erection. Forty-eight to seventy-two hours is what they claim.

WHAT?

Are there really men out there willing to walk around like that for two or three days in a row? I mean sheesh, there's so many walls or chairs or tables you could bump into with a protrusion such as this. And hey, there ain't no wiener bandages for an injury incurred while trying to cut a corner. And hells bells, what if you accidentally run into a small child. That could lead to all kinds of legal repercussions.

I mean how can this stuff be safe? Does it come with a side order of nitroglycerin for your heart? I've seen all those televised ads for Cialis and Viagra. They're always warning about "if you have an erection longer than four hours" you should go see your doctor immediately. Hell, with this particular product, if your doctor isn't female and horny, what's the point of seeing them?

I think what makes their ad's particularly appealing to a great many consumers out there is that you can get absolutely shit-faced drunk and this stuff, 'viagpure', will still have the desired effect. Better yet, it claims it can save a failing marriage, and can make your sperm shoot farther and with more precision than an arrow leaving a spear gun.

Hellooooo!

Is the distance sperm can shoot something we give a lot of thought to? Hmm! Did I miss this part of the lecture in health class? I guess I may have to ponder on whether there are actually any benefits to this.

Now unless you're a famous golfer claiming 'hole in ones' all the time—I don't see the point of using a product such as this. Or maybe, just once, for two or three days, I would 'get' the point then wonder—what's the point?

It's already bad enough that I don't get enough sleep. I can't imagine staying up for that many hours in a row just to wreak the benefits of this man enhancer—nor would I want to!

And what about the kids?

Don't you think they'd wonder where we were for those three days even though we were home the whole time? And how would we explain the bags under our eyes, and the fact that, once we did emerge from wherever we'd hidden away, certain parts of our body would no longer function as they once had? That we both actually might need some kind of medical intervention.

I don't know, call me old-fashioned. I love a good romp in the hay, but I don't think Ms. Vagina would be as acceptable to participating in this kind of marathon sex any more.

Of course this would all boil down to whether I actually gave in to one of those middle of the night commercials I told you about earlier. You know…for VD–vaginal dryness. Maybe this is where that old adage comes in–*the squeaky wheel gets the grease.*

I've known a few men during my lifetime who proclaim they can go at it all night, but seventy-two hours under the best of circumstances seems, well, a little excessive to me–for anything.

I can't help thinking that with all the blood running down there to keep that sinking ship alive, what the hell is keeping the rest of the boat floating? Doesn't the rest of the body need some of that blood? But then again, women have always said that a man thinks with his dick, so maybe the brain is getting exactly all the blood it needs. I don't know—call me crazy.

I say forget about a drug that keeps it up like the energizer bunny and instead, just get one of those miniature life alert bracelets and attach it directly to the penis. You let your imagination run wild until a situation 'arises', the life alert goes off, and whammo!

"Oh honey….did you hear that?"

"Hear what?"

"It's beeping."

"Oh…I thought that was the oven timer."

"No, it's me, hurry up, and turn off the oven. We've got about two minutes."

"But it's a soufflé, it'll deflate without the heat."

"Yeah, well…SO WILL THIS."

Maybe I'm just old. I do not want to have sex for seventy-two hours in a row, nor do my hipbones.

Let's be real here.

If you have the ability to stay awake for several days in a row, you're probably still in your twenties and don't need this shit anyway. If you're an alcoholic in a failing marriage, hello, it's probably not lack of sex that's causing your marriage to fail.

$\mathcal{T}$ WELVE

Sexy Grey Hair...

...looks absolutely fantastic on some people. It gives them an air of wisdom, an air of maturity, and sometimes an air of mystery, but for me, it's just a sign of what's come and gone. It's a sign of getting old.

I was blessed with a thick mop of brunette hair. Thank god for the little things, right? I got the hair gene from my mother's side I think. (This makes up for her not giving me the green thumb). She's always had thick hair and still does, and guess what? At eighty-years-old, there's still not one strand of grey to be found on her head. My dad, well, not so much. He ended up with one of those Nero like rings of silver hair that started just above his ear and ended just above his ear. The rest of his balding head was fodder for many sunscreen debates.

I love, love, love my long tresses, as does my husband. Doesn't matter if I'm staying home, going to the gym, or going to the grocery store– my hair is always washed and blown out into my usual style, unless of course it's one of 'those medusa' days whereupon I don a baseball cap. You know—the bad hair day where no gel or cream will tame it.

Okay so I've been in a hair rut for thirty some years but it seems to work for me. I think it's my way of pretending that time has not slipped through my hands.

I always wonder when I run into someone I haven't seen in a long time and they say, "you look exactly like you did twenty years ago". I'm never quite sure whether I should take this as a compliment, that I have aged well, or, are they referring to the fact that I'm stuck in a rut. Hmm?

There are some things that change in our lives, like the location of our boobs and butts cheeks, our expanding waistline, and our ability to stay awake past nine o'clock, but hair, well that's something we can still control.

Jacqui Brown

My motto is 'there will nary be a grey hair on my head'. I just can't let it happen! That 'au natural' thing is not for me. I've tried to go blonde once or twice but I could never live up to the jokes.

I've always said that, when it comes to the telltale signs of aging, I'm going to go down hard. Hubby likes that I think this way. I know I've said this out loud a few times because this always seems to make his ears perk up if he happens to hear me. Yeah, you guessed right, the boner thing again. What is with that man?

Sometimes I'll be talking to a friend on the phone about this very subject unaware that he's within listening distance. As soon as I hang up, sometimes even before I hang up, he'll come strutting into the room with '*that*' look on his face and a very obvious protrusion in his pants.

"Remind me to starch those pants," I say in response to the Thunder Down Under.

He can see that I've already busied myself with whatever I was doing.

"Oh, okay," he says shoving his hands in his pockets. Both his upper and lower posture changes and he slowly retreats to the other room. Poor baby!

What I want to know is why this grey hair never just flows into your regular hair? Mine always looks like bionic pubic hair on crack. It points straight up towards the sky, gleaming like a beacon screaming, *"look at me, look at me!"*

I remember going Christmas shopping a few years back. I was at one of those large discount stores standing near a bin of 'whatever', when I noticed a mirrored wall directly behind it. Being somewhat vain, I looked up to catch a glimpse of myself because I thought I'd looked reasonably hot when I left the house that morning. Instead, I was devastated to see this one lousy grey hair in its gravity defying position.

Yep, it was like someone had rubbed a balloon on the top of my head to create that magnetic weirdness. It was crinkled and white as hell. It was about three inches tall, and it stood out like a sore thumb against the chestnut of the rest of my glorious mane. It shone like a neon sign under those horrid fluorescent lights.

I remember this lovely older woman sidling up beside me at the same time I'd made this discovery.

"Do you see that?" I asked her.

"See what?" she says.

"That," I said.

"What," she asked.

"That hair," I said.

"Oh it's lovely dear. Hair is good!" she said.

"What's so lovely about it?" I asked.

"It looks good on you I'm sure," she replied.

"How does that look good?" I queried.

"It's hair…it looks good," she replied.

"What…are you blind?" I said.

DEAD SILENCE…

I actually turned to look at her. Of course this is when I notice the turban and the dark glasses she's wearing.

I look down, and yes, there it is…the fucking seeing eye dog. Yep, he's got the vest and everything.

"Maybe you should buy a hat to cover them asshole?" she said calling on the dog to lead her away from me.

CRAP!

Once again, I need to open my mouth and change feet!

This, of course, put an end to my festive shopping. Instead I headed to the drug store for hair dye.

Standing in front of the mirror in my bathroom an hour later, my head smeared with dark cream, I leaned forward to take a gander at my eyebrows.

There it was!

CRAP!

One little grey motherfucker sticking out away from the natural path of the others. Only this kind of close-up inspection would reveal such a betrayer. I reached up, stuck my finger into the shiny hair dye and dabbed it onto both my eyebrows. I stood there looking like a Harpo Marx stand in waiting for the timer to ring out telling me that youth had been restored. That I was once again in full youthful bloom.

That was when another thought hit me.

Oh no! What about…?

I had my first Brazilian later that day!

$\mathcal{T}$HIRTEEN

$\mathcal{M}$ating $\mathcal{S}$eason...

...happens in the early spring most of the time.

You got the birds and the bees, the dogs and cats, as well as a large population of various domestic and wild animals doing *it*. *It* is such a natural phenomena that it usually passes unnoticed, with the exception of those pain in the ass cats who howl and scream at each other in the wee hours of the night demanding submission from their partner.

— Jacqui Brown —

I'll tell you this much, if someone screamed at me that way in order to have sex, the last thing they'd be getting is *IT*! I'd clamp my legs together so tight it'd take a crew with crowbars to separate them. As a matter of fact, I'd be off and running because if they scream at you before sex, God only knows what's going to happen later on down the road.

These are signs that must not be ignored people.

But interestingly enough, I've discovered that Los Angeles has a human mating season that runs year round. This kind of mating doesn't take place in the bedroom either—oddly enough, it takes place on the surface streets, in parking lots, and wherever else people and cars mix.

Here in Los Angeles there are millions of cars on the road at any given time of the day. Even in the wee hours of the morning you can see the stream of headlights moving along the freeway like a trail of lava. Where everybody's going at that time is anybody's guess. Maybe they're going to work or coming home from work. Maybe they're out partying, or maybe they're just flat out wasting gas going nowhere just because they're bored. They're out there morning, noon, and night.

By my estimates about 10% of these road warriors are seniors, 75% are the money-makers—you know—us—the baby boomers, the shakers and the movers, and last but not least are the 15% who fall into the teenagers/young adult group.

This last group of course is the most worrisome. Not that we don't have to worry about some of those seniors out there who have trouble discerning which is the gas or brake peddle, or the baby boomer whose financial empire is about to fail and they've got six tons of metal and chrome to vent with—I'm still most uncomfortable with the teen/young adult group.

They're so technologically user friendly. It's rare to see one of them driving without a phone clamped in the palms of their hands trying to talk, text, or photograph whomever or whatever strikes their fancy while traveling at high speed.

From my experience this usually always takes place right next to my car. And, oh, by the way, if you don't see the phone in their hands, you should be especially careful because that means they may have dropped it on the floor and will likely start swerving about in order to retrieve this precious communication system.

What worries me even more is that they also seem to be searching for love on the road. I've seen it first hand, this banter that goes on between drivers who happen to catch each other's eyes.

Now, don't get me wrong. I'm all for looking for love—but while you're driving? Come on people! This does not seem to me when you should be doing anything but keeping your eyes on the road with your hands placed precisely at the ten o'clock/two o'clock position ON THE STEERING WHEEL.

Jacqui Brown

I guess this shouldn't surprise me that much because the world has become this big pulsing beat that's so fast paced. If you don't have a hold of the knot at the end of the rope, well, you're in big trouble. You'll be so left behind your kids will wander around aimlessly with that world famous question—*where's mommy?*

Of course dad, who's kept pace with technology all along as it progressed, will then in turn have to tell them that mom missed the boat.

She's lost somewhere between the 80's and the 90's.

He'll then explain that she picked up the computer far too late, that she can only think of a Blackberry as something you make pies with, and once you tell her East or West instead of left or right, there's a good possibility she may never be seen again.

Hell, this world's so fast and easy you don't even have to get out of your car at Starbucks any more. Yep, you can just drive through and never waste one precious moment of freeway time. True Starbuckian's cruise around the building at a snails pace, but the very second that cup is in their hands, they peel out of there like their pants are on fire. Yes, we Angelinos' love the coffee God!

Anyway, I got caught up in one of these mating sessions the other day after I dropped my son off at school. There I was, just sitting there, minding my own business, when this young girl pulled up next to me. She stopped just slightly ahead of me, but I could still see her perfectly clear through the back passenger door window. I guessed her to be somewhere in her late teens or early twenties. She's got her hair tied up in that, *I'm too lazy to wash my hair knot* on the top of her head. I recognize this knot instantly because my daughter wears this same style most of the time. I've named it the sumo roll for obvious reasons. Okay, so I can't exactly tell what she looks like but she's probably cuter than I think. It's hard to tell from my vantage point because her face is covered by the biggest pair of sunglasses I've ever seen. I mean really, these things were so big you could barely make out any of her facial features. They seem a little excessive size wise, but maybe this is how she saves on sun block.

Her car, well, it's not so much a car than it is pieces of metal screwed together, and it appears to have been, at one point, some shade of blue. My guess is she's an avid driver-texter by the amount of damage I can see just on this side of the car. Oddly enough, I also notice a small patch of grass hanging down from the bottom of what once was a shiny chrome bumper. What she had in place of the factory authorized safety device, now looked more like tin foil that had been used, scrunched up, and then recycled in the form of a bumper. This bumper misfortune must have been fairly recent too because the grass is still showing signs of life. It's probably due to the fact that there's a tiny sprinkler head peaking its head out of the patch and it's still dripping water.

What a lucky little sod!

Now, I'm curious about the interior of her car. I roll forward a little, just enough to snoop but not so obvious she'll turn to look at me. The back seat is covered with piles of clothes, water bottles, empty coffee cups, empty cigarette packages, and a bunch of other things that I can't actually recognize. This is what I'd call the typical teenage car. I know it like the back of my hand. I've got one just like it sitting in my driveway at home.

I notice that not only is she chewing gum, she's also got a freshly lit cigarette hanging from her lips. Her fingers are flying across the keyboard of her phone at the speed of light for what seems like the worlds longest message composed on a cell phone. Finally she sets the phone on the dashboard for a brief moment and removes the cigarette from between her lips. I see a pink bubble squish out through her somewhat over plumped lips, and when it pops, there's a small cloud of smoke that lingers in front of her. Holy crap!

I'm thinking that if there was ever an award for personal multi-tasking while driving, this girl takes the cake.

On the other side of my car, I see a brand new shiny white BMW pull up just slightly ahead of my car. This one is driven by a boy who looks to be twenty something as well. I watch as he looks at the girl across the one lane span. I see that he's trying to get her attention, so like any good voyeur, I crack the windows on both sides of my car so I can hear them.

"Hey," he calls out to her tapping his horn just a little to make sure he gets her attention.

It takes her a minute to respond. She reaches over, turns the radio down, and yells back "what's up."

"Wanna hang out?" he yells.

"No," she says and rolls up the passenger side window.

Flash forward to the next light where we're still aligned in the same way. I notice both her windows are down again. This is the beauty of living in California. Even in the winter we can drive around with our windows down.

He taps the horn in another attempt to get her attention, then yells out his single greeting of 'hey', but this time it's a little louder.

She sees him again and turns the radio down.

"WHAT?" she says now somewhat annoyed.

"Can I call you?" he yells back as he waves his cell phone towards her.

She shakes her head no.

"Come on we'll have fun, maybe we can go smoke some hookah," he says hoping this will entice her. This of course is a dead giveaway in regards to his ancestral ethnic heritage.

"Where do you live?" she responds.

"I live with my folks...er...I mean, I live in Hollywood," he says stuttering, trying to cover up his faux pas.

She smiles the most beautiful smile at him showing off her perfect teeth, then her window starts to go up.

I look back at him and he's got his hands up in the air as if to say WTF. He tries one last honk, but the light changes. She flips him off even though she's still got that big smile on her face, then makes a left hand turn. He chucks his phone down on to the seat and speeds away.

So I'm thinking to myself, I wonder if this actually ever works?

About ten minutes later I pull up to another of the million lights I'll get caught at on my way home. Sitting beside me is a kind of gruff looking young man. He looks to be around my daughter's age. I decide to try out my own version of car mating just for the hell of it.

I roll down my window, tap my horn and wait for a response. Nothing! So this time I blast the horn. Well that gets his bloody attention now doesn't it, and he rolls down the window. His radio is so loud I have to shout.

"Hey, you wanna hang out smoke some hookah?" I ask even though I'm wondering what I'll actually do if he says okay.

"WHAT?" he screams back at me.

"Wanna go smoke some hookah?" I yell back.

He looks at me, then looks out his driver's side window to make sure that I'm not talking to someone else, then turns back to me.

"No ma'am, I don't. Jesus Christ! Aren't you a little old for this?" he yells at me then shuts the window. Now he's staring at me like I'm a complete idiot.

Cut me like a fucking knife that little bastard did when the word 'ma'am' rolled out of his puckered chapped lips.

For one brief moment I consider my choices. I could ignore his fucking slanderous ignorance, or I could ram him with my SUV.

But I persisted. This *was* just a game after all.

I wave my cell phone at him, then make the 'call me' gesture. I wait with bated breath for his response.

His window rolls down. I hold my breath a little longer.

"Get away from me lady," he screams.

I ignore his protest and mouth the words 'call me' one last time.

The light changes, he sticks his hand out the driver side window, flips me off, then speeds away leaving a little rubber behind to show his disgust that some old woman just hit on him.

So, I rethink what went wrong. Maybe I have to try this with—someone more my age. Someone who won't be so disrespectful.

I spot my next victim about two lights later and man, this guy's good looking, the real deal, the schnizzle to my schnazzle. You know the type; suit, broad shoulders, dark glasses, just a hint of 5 o'clock shadow, briefcase lying on the passenger seat, bitchin' car. I actually felt my nipples get hard in anticipation.

I roll up next to him and see his windows are down.

"Hey...wanna hang out, smoke some hookah?" I yell through the open window.

"Pardon me?" he says like he didn't hear exactly what I said.

"Come on, let's go smoke some hookah," I yell back even louder so there's no way he won't hear me.

He looks me over, shakes his head, waves me off with his hand, then rolls up his window. He's intentionally ignoring me by pretending to watch for the light to change. I tap the horn one last time, but this time, when he looks at me I've already got my hand in that telephone position, you know, thumb and pinky pressed to my ear and I yell out 'call me'. He rolls his eyes and makes a dash out of there even though the light's still red.

Oh well, I think to myself. It was a fun experiment. That's when *I* hear the loud blast of a horn.

I glance over at the car that was next to good-looking guy and see this old Armenian man ogling me. Actually, I can't decipher if it's a leer or an ogle, but either way, this guy looks like a piece of work. My guess would be he's maybe seventy, seventy-five. He's actually waving a big red hookah pipe at me and nodding his head in the yes motion, all while moving his bushy eyebrow up and down in that weird little come hither motion. I see he's got a front tooth missing, and he's a little short in the hair area, and I believe he's wearing one of those blue plaid matching shirt and short sets, which means he's probably also wearing white knee high socks with dress shoes.

CRAP!!!!

I train my eyes back on the light praying it will change. I roll my window up to block out whatever he's yelling at me because I can't understand what he's saying anyway as he spews out in his native language.

That right there was enough to put an end to my little experiment.

As I headed towards home to hubby, I felt eternally grateful that I didn't actually have to pursue this ever again.

Oddly enough, about two hours later, in walks my daughter carrying a rather large box.

"Mom, wait till you see what I just bought!" she says more excited than I've seen her in a long time.

"What is it?" I ask.

"Just wait a second!" she says.

She gets a knife from the drawer, slits open the top of the box and pulls out a bright red Hookha Pipe.

I guess she's dating again!

FOURTEEN

Baby Fat...

...is something that all women have to deal with after that freaking blessed event of allowing a far too large object to slide out of the smallest portal on our body!

Let's face it girls. We really don't give much thought to our expanding girth when it's under the guise of 'baby fat'. As that little sucker grows inside of us, we cling to that self-serving deception tactic of "I've got to feed the baby" or "I'm trying to protect the baby" with all this added cushion.

B-U-L-L-S-H-I-T!

Pregnancy brain makes us delusional is what I think.

That all we've really done is stuffed our bloody faces until we look like we're ready to explode because we think no one is really watching our weight, they're only watching the blessed progression of a developing baby.

So, flash forward.

You realize your kids are nearly adults now and you're still carrying around a pile of flab that's been there since way back when.

With the recession like it is now, so many of us are left to our own devices to get in shape because gym memberships are still at a premium. The price of working out one-on-one with a personal trainer is also out of reach for most of us now, and you already know that it didn't go so well the last time I tried it, so what do we do? We start looking around to find the cheapest possible way to get the most for our money.

Hubby and I usually walk every morning at our local park. If we go around the outside twice we can get in about two miles. Unfortunately, when it's a little cooler outside, we take a shortcut so we can stay in the sun. Hello…short cuts will not get rid of said baby fat.

But the good part is, we'd find new inspiration during these little treks because every day we'd see different groups working out. You've got your boot camps, your one-on-ones, basketball games, soccer games, joggers…there's a plethora of people trying to get fit, or as I like to think of it– getting your Jell-O to finally set.

One group I'd noticed over the past year is made up of several young mothers and their toddlers. They use their strollers for balance, use their kids as free weights, and all in all, they seem like they're having a good time instead of just sweating their asses off all alone. They've got that camaraderie going on. From the look on their faces, they really don't seem to mind the stretching, crunching, or jogging so long as they can do it together.

The more I think about it, the more it makes sense. You grab a bunch of your 'baby-fat' friends who are stuck at home with their young children and you work out together. It's the perfect world–like minded women at the same place in their life, all trying to work off the same fat.

So, after pondering this idea week after week, I finally got brave enough to go ask them if it was an open group, and how much did it cost to join.

"We don't pay anything, we just work out together because it's more fun to do it this way," says the girl who kind of looks like she's leading the group. Or maybe it's just that her ass is so big she's the one person who really stands out in the group.

"Oh," I said. That's definitely a plus.

But then I notice that they're all kind of staring at me in that odd kind of way because it's obvious I'm a lot older than all of them.

"Could I come?" I ask.

"Well...you're...I think you're a little old for our group," she says as she looks me up and down with that smug superior look on her face.

Do I say anything about her fat ass in defense of her geriatric remark—NO!

I want to bitch-slap her though, but I refrain from doing so because this might be my ticket to shed a few pounds without spending a dime, so I stand there, steadfast in my cool, calm, collected way.

"No...I don't think I'm too old," I say as I crush the urge to take this bitch down right then and there. "I'm not as old as I look you know."

The whole pack of them exchange a look. You know the one. I can see each and every one of them trying to formulate a reason to get me to go away.

"Do you have kids?" she asks, at the same time I see her surveying my waistline.

BITCH PLEASE!

I want to yell at her, but I bite my tongue instead.

I'm pretty sure she can see the daggers flying out

of my eyeballs right towards her heart.

"Yeah! I've got kids. Two as a matter of fact," I reply waiting to see where she's going to go next.

She looks around at the others in the group trying to surmise by the looks on their faces whether or not she should offer me a place in the group. They pull themselves into a little huddle and have a short conference. A moment later they separate and fat ass takes another long look at me.

"Why don't you come Wednesday...with your kid," she says. "We'll see if you can keep up with us."

OH NO YOU DIDN'T GIRL!

I can't believe she went there so fast!

Yep, she upped the ante by attacking my competitive side.

Oh well, maybe this was exactly what I needed to hear to motivate me to undo what time and gluttony had done to me.

"Okie-dokie, I'll see you Wednesday then," I say.

I can hear them giggling as I walk away.

But then it dawns on me. I may have actually bitten off more than I could chew! As a matter of fact, I know I have, because for the next few moments as I walk towards my car, I have to maneuver my now aching tongue around so I can dislodge that little piece of it I bit off, the piece that has now become stuck in my back molar.

So here's one of the *only* perks of home schooling. My son is constantly available, and fortunately for me, he has the same warped humor that I do. I know he'll be game for this, and beside, he loves to work out too, so it's game on.

Tuesday rolls around and I go to my neighbor and ask if I can borrow her jogger stroller.

"What do you need it for," she asks.

I lie, telling her I'm going to be babysitting a friends kid on Wednesday.

"Oh, okay," she says.

Wednesday morning, I get up early, wash my hair do my makeup, and dress in my best workout clothes. I'm not going to let these girls see the real morning me under any circumstances!

I get my son up, feed him so he won't get cranky, and we head off to the park.

When I pull into the parking lot, I can see them off in the distance. There's five or six of them today and their already stretching, while at the same time sucking back the last drops of their coffee.

I get the stroller out of the back of my car, set it on the ground, and then try to open it.

CRAP!

I guess we should have done a run through at home.

I realize it has some kind of dam fangled lock on it somewhere but I just can't find it. I look around in desperation, and like a mirage before my eyes, there appears another health nut, another mother, with her kid, in the same kind of stroller, and I know she's not part of the mommy group I'm about to join. She sees my plight and comes to my aid.

She flicks a little toggle and the God damn buggy springs to life just like when you pull the toggle of the life jacket on an airplane. Oh yeah! That'll be a story for another time!

I jump out of the way and she laughs at me.

"Sometimes these things have a life of their own," she offers. "They take some getting used to."

"No shit!" I say thinking these things must be manufactured by Toyota because of the speed at which they open.

The smile on her lips turns sour and she glares at me.

I slap my hand over my mouth.

My bad!

I look down at her beautiful four or five year old little girl who's also staring at me now.

"I'm sooooo sorry…that just kind of slipped out," I say trying to salvage my bad self. The self that is foul mouthed when least expected.

She says nothing in return for my apology. She just turns away and heads off with an air of indignation. I watch as they get back on the path and I'm pretty sure I see her sweet little daughter's hand dart out from the side of the stroller to flip me off.

My son looks at me and we both burst out laughing.

Okay, so now we've got the stroller ready for loading. I look at my son then look at the stroller and wonder how this is going to work.

At six-feet-four inches this is definitely going to be interesting.

Knowing that my son's in pretty good shape I figure we should be all right. It might take a minute or two to finagle his long limbed extremities into it—but come hell or high water— it was going to happen!

My pride and mid-life fat was on the line here.

After ten minutes of pushing, shoving, contorting, and cramming his gangly body parts this way and that, he was sufficiently trapped in the damn blasted contraption.

Was he a happy camper? No!

"I can't breathe," he said. "My balls hurt!"

"Oh shut up you big baby," I said slamming the sunshade down over his head.

Then it hit me. This was so uber-perfect because he was acting like a two-year-old already.

I win!

As I approach the group, I am met with stares, glares, and more of those what the fuck looks they'd given me on my initial approach a few days earlier.

But I flash my pearly white teeth at them. I'm still winning at this point.

They never mentioned anything about the child's age limit—their loss—my gain!

"You didn't say anything about your son being...well...older," Miss Fat Ass says.

"You never asked," I say smugly because I know she can't think of one damn thing to come back with.

I could see a couple of these young girls *checking out* my son and it brought a smile to my lips. He's pretty damn cute if I don't say so myself. He's tall for his age, so I'm pretty sure there's a few gutter thoughts breezing through one or two of these young mother's minds. But you know what? I don't mind so much as long as they let me work out with them...*for free*!

Oh the sacrifice's we mother's make to save a dime here and there.

"Well, let's just start then," Miss FA says.

We're starting out with squats. Ah geeze! Here we go again. Not once while I was checking them out did I ever see them doing squats! Oh well. I decide to go with the flow. Now here's where having my son in the stroller pays off big time though.

I can see that these young girls are really going to have to use their leg muscles in order not to tip over their strollers as they use them to keep their balance. I watch as they check the safety straps and harnesses that will keep their little ones safe and sound.

My son is an anchor for me. His hundred and seventy five pounds of lean muscle hunkering down in that stroller means that I can disperse the muscle usage equally between my double chinned arms and my less than toned legs.

"Just hang on dude," I warn him because the straps on this stroller are unusable because of his size.

He unfurls his thirty-six inch inseam legs, adjusts his balls, and then pushes the sunshade away so he can watch me. I hear the first hint of a giggle sneaking out of him because he knows this is my least favorite exercise and I really, really have to concentrate so I don't start laughing.

Miss FA starts the drill.

"One. Hold it. Two. Hold it. Don't forget to breathe," she barks out like a drill sargeant.

During the second squat, I start to feel that old familiar gurgle that emanates from my five-decade-old gas pipes.

Give me a break God! Please!

Remember: Mid-life and squats are not the best combination for me, especially with the absence of Gas-X . That's what got me into this situation in the first place.

I take a deep breath and squeeze the old sphincter muscle as tight as I can in hopes that I can avoid the possibility of my butt actually erupting, again, in public!

Oops!

There goes the first warning shot! I count my blessings immediately because there's no obvious noise.

Smell…Well that's another thing. Thank God I was down wind.

Dipping for number three felt a little better. I guess

the warning shot had relieved enough pressure to let me continue without fear.

Wrong!

When I finally get all the way down—my butt, which has acquired it's own life cycle, decided it was time to party. Oh yeah…bells and whistles—drum roll please—it was time to blow the party horn. The best I could hope for is that it wouldn't react like a piñata actually spilling its guts.

"Wow, this feels fantastic," I scream at the top of my lungs hoping it will drown out the sound of the thunderous blasphemy that seems to be taking its time exiting the building.

Of course my outburst is greeted with more WTF stares. I fight fire with fire and stare back. I don't really care because, if I had my druthers, I'd rather they think I was a crazy old bitch instead of a stinking rotten smelly one.

I'd been so worried about the noise I didn't notice that the wind had changed direction.

My first hint that the odor had hit home was when my son clutched, first his nose, then his throat before making that gagging face over and over. About five seconds later he keeled over and played dead.

One of the girls noticed him slumped over while he was playing possum and pointed towards him.

"Is he okay?" she said with real concern in her voice.

"Oh yes, he'll be fine in a minute," I assure her.

I kick the bottom of the stroller to get my point across, to tell him to quit it. If he blows this for me, there'd be a steep price to pay later.

That's when he throws in a full body twitch just to make sure he gets his point across—that being that I'd nearly killed him as last night's broccoli regurgitated itself. I guess there's only so much a person can do to reign in our personal carbon footprint. Obviously, I haven't got a clue!

"He just needs a little fresh air," I say and start squatting again.

"Noooooooo…!"

It comes out of his mouth like a little childish whisper.

"Oh My God! Don't do it mom, please!" he says seeing me preparing to do the fourth squat.

"Can you just shut the Hell up?" I hiss at him as I ignore the hint of tears in his eyes. "You don't see any of the other kids making a scene."

"Hello…what are they, six months old…a year? If that smell reaches any of them you might face a murder charge you know!" he says in his own defense.

I look over at their sweet little faces. They look like little angels 'now' and all I can do is smile. These young mother's have no idea what's to come ten, fifteen years from now.

No sooner do these words leave his lips when I see the air start to ripple towards them. I've got about two seconds to come up with something clever because they all know I'm now up wind. I see it hit them like a sledgehammer.

One of the girls screams out, *Oh My God! What on earth is that stink?*

They've all clamped their hands over their noses in the only defensive position they've got. They all turn towards me and stare. Now, since I'm standing behind my son, he cannot see that I'm pointing at him with one hand and waving my other hand under my nose. I see him strike a particularly handsome expression on his face as he notices all the girls staring at him. All I can hope for is that he doesn't turn around and see that I am letting him take the fall for my bad ass.

Miss FA calls off the squats, then announces that we're now going to jog around the park twice.

Oh Lordy!

I knew I should have quit smoking a long time ago.

My mind starts to reel as I anticipate the possibility of respiratory failure. I know if I keep a fairly slow pace I can probably do it. I am comforted by the fact that I can see the giant hospital sign directly across the street from the park. I'm sure that if anything happens, like me going face down, the six of them can surely drag my sorry fat ass across the grass and deposit me in the emergency room in a timely manner.

The six of them take off leaving me in a heap of dust.

I watch their perky little asses and am fascinated by the fact that they don't flop up and down like mine. Well, the one exception to that is Ms. FA. She'd got me way beat in the Gluteus Maximus area.

Before I can even think about running, we have to reconfigure my son's legs back into the stroller so we don't get tripped up and end up on a gurney for other reasons.

Okay. He's finally in and we're off and running. It's not as bad as I thought it was going to be, except for the fact that I can't remember the last time I ran anywhere while trying to push a combined weight of say two-hundred pounds!

My son decides he'll help out by unfurling his legs and straddling the stroller trying to run along with me. Each time his foot hits the ground however, the stroller zigs in the opposite direction and we end up looking like we're RWD...running while drunk, which actually, I have a faint recollection of doing once.

"Put your damn feet up," I yell at him. "You're gonna kill us both."

"I can't, you have to stop first."

"No way Jose," I say looking over my shoulder. The girls are about to lap me.

He somehow pulls his legs up to his chest and holds them there with his arms so we can keep moving. I try desperately to keep ahead of them, but it's no use.

One by one they zoom past.

Fucking kids!

I hate failure!

Try as I might...I cannot keep up. Plan B starts to formulate in my befuddled, not enough morning coffee, too much wine last night, brain. I can see the group is about to round the last corner of the track, the home stretch, and realize that if I don't act now, I'll have to go down in defeat. I FUCKING HATE LOSING!

I tell my son to get out of the stroller so we can cut across the center of the track. If I time this right, not only will this put us ahead of them, it'll also give me enough time to squish him back into the stroller and build up a little sweat.

When the girls finally 'catch up' with us they look confused.

"I know…I know, you didn't even see me pass you huh?" I say pretending to be breathless. "Evelyn Wood's speed running…took that course last year."

This seems to impress them, or at least this is what I tell myself.

Really, all I want to do is sit down, slug back some water, have a smoke, and rest for about an hour.

No such luck. Apparently this workout group works like a 'real' boot camp. No rest for the weary or the old.

This really blows! How come I didn't notice the ferocity of their regime during my walks? Guess that boils down to the old adage of 'you only see what you want to see!' But then again, this is probably why miss FA's boobs are still perky, and why her ass, even in its grand form, doesn't budge as much as I thought it would. Guess I've been out of the loop a little too long.

Miss FA barks out that we're about to use the children as free weights so we should unleash them from their stroller seat.

I gasp! My son sighs!

We're instructed to lie on our backs, pull our legs up to a fetal position, and then place our child up onto the lower part of our legs so we can do calisthenic leg lifts.

As I lie there, on my back, looking up towards the sky, I see the evil smirk on my son's face. It dawns on me that I should have brought a towel or something to lay on because now my back will be scratchy all day as the dead grass penetrates my t-shirt.

"Wipe that stupid smile off your face son, this is serious business," I hiss at him.

"Oh I know. I can't wait to see how this works out," he says getting down on his knees.

He maneuvers his chest onto my lower legs. About two seconds later, as his dead weight hits home, I feel all the air in my lungs disappear.

OMG!

Where oh where had my lower body strength gone?

I'm the handy man/woman of the house! I've framed in walls, built fences, framed out and built concrete stairs, hung drywall, plastered walls, moved two tons of pebbles, sand and rocks, planted trees out of their twenty four inch boxes, changed tires on cars, hauled fifty gallon buckets of paint, reworked plumbing, and GAVE BIRTH TWICE—VAGINALLY.

How was it that this had not strengthened my legs? Why was this hundred and seventy-five pound punk suffocating me?

I looked to my left then my right, and each one of these girls was breezing through the routine. Well no shit! They were balancing maybe thirteen or fifteen pounds at the most.

Miss FA is glaring at me by this time. I'm sure she's formulating the words she's going to say to me after all is said and done that will make me go away and let them get on with their business of getting fit.

My son is looking down at me with that 'what are you going to do now' look, and all I can do is smile.

"You know, you could help me out here you little peckerhead! Put your hands on the ground and take some of the pressure off," I say to him.

"But mom…that would be cheating wouldn't it?"

He says this not knowing that these words were, in reality, a death wish on his part.

"Sweetheart, if you don't help me out here your gonads might just meet up with an unsightly accident," I say smiling through gritted teeth.

"Oh," he says as the smile evaporates from his lips.

He realizes that he's in a compromised position. He lowers his hands to the ground in self-defense.

Okie-dokie then! In this position I can actually lift

him. We manage to get about ten leg lifts done. Just as I really start to get the rhythm down, Miss FA says we're done.

She stands up and sets her oh so sweet daughter down in the middle of the circle with the other toddlers. She looks over at me, smiles her movie star smile, and I start to wonder whether or not my family can sue her for unnecessary cruelty in the event that I actually drop dead from exertion.

I know she can see the sweat pouring off me like Niagara Falls, and that my face must be red as an apple at this point, but she doesn't say a word—but then nor do I. It's just another moment where I want to bitch slap her for pushing me to, or rather, beyond my limit.

I chant silently to myself. I am older and wiser and she is not going to win! I am older and wiser, I am older...

I need to gather myself here. I pull my t-shirt up so I can swab away some of the fluids that have leaked out of me. Not a good move on my part because now they all see the body sucker I've been sporting under my clothes to reveal only my curvy side.

OOPS!

I can see them staring at me. Yep! There were twelve eyes bearing down on my girdled midriff.

"I have a bad back. I need the pressure to hold my

spine in place," I say in my defense returning my t-shirt to where it should have never left.

This is going to hell in a basket!

Miss FA rolls her eyes back in her head. I imitate her so she's fully aware that I am not going to let her throw me. She announces that she'll stay with the children while we go free jog.

What? Free jog? What the fuck is that? She can't be serious! That last stint nearly killed me even at the piddly-assed pace I tried to maintain. If I have to move faster than that, which I assumed she would want us to, I might never see my family again.

My son plopped down amid the toddlers and waved me off. I hurled my keys at him hoping to strike something significant, but he's quick. He ducked and the keys landed in the only wet spot in the park.

"Go on mom, don't worry about me," he said, right before he burst out laughing.

I put one foot in front of the other and made my way back to the track. Without the distraction of the added weight (my son and the stroller) I figured I could ace this portion of the workout for at least for one lap—maybe even two.

Unfortunately, my boobs had other plans. I don't know why I hadn't thought about doubling up on the sports bra, I just know that I hadn't. Big mistake!

I was now being bitch-slapped by my own flesh.

The girls had turned into out of control slinky's—undulating up and down, side-to-side—stretching in ways that could, in no way, be considered flattering, nor could it be in their best interest health wise. I slowed down in order to stop this hideous circus act. I hadn't even reached the second turn on the track when two of the young mothers lapped me.

SON OF A BITCH!

I did the only thing I could.

I stopped.

I made my way back to the center of the track.

With my shoulders slumped in defeat, I headed directly to Miss FA.

"You win! I'm done."

"But we're just getting started," she says flashing her Chiclet-white smile.

BITCH PLEASE!

I'm so tired I can't even be witty. I glare at my son, who's currently mimicking the other toddlers by sucking his thumb. I have just enough wherewithal to pull my shoulders back and stand as proud as I can.

"Let's go son," I say.

"Where we going mama?"

"To lick my wounds!"

Just as we finish packing everything back into the car, I happen to catch sight of a group of seniors doing Thai Chi under the shade of several giant eucalyptus trees right next to the parking lot.

I've already been duped once so I need to see for myself that this tame looking group is not suddenly going to break into some racy hip-hop moves or ridiculous bone/muscle/lung defying cardio action that will completely end me.

But none of that happens. They stay true to the slow and meditative movements.

"Ah-so young grasshopper," I say smiling at my son. "There is a God after all—I'll be right back."

$\mathcal{F}$IFTEEN

$\mathcal{L}$ibido $\mathcal{B}$oosters...

...have become big business these days. So many people I know have had to resort to them in order to maintain any kind of sex life.

Where the hell have all the lost libido's gone I wonder?

Where was mine? Was it lost in the same vacuum

as all those missing socks I've failed to locate after doing laundry?

Did it fall out that day I wore granny panties instead of my thong? If that's the case, I should have known better. I knew the elastic was loose.

Or did it escape when they ripped out my innards to protect me from the blob that had taken over my uterus back in my forties?

Could it have snuck out while I was sleeping one night with my legs spread haphazardly in the nine o'clock/three o'clock position hoping for one of those rare, did I say rare, I think I said rare, spontaneous orgasms.

I think it's more likely I lost it somewhere between packing lunches, running to the dry cleaners, washing, drying, and folding endless loads of laundry, dropping the kids off wherever then picking them up later, homeschooling my son, (kill me now) paying the bills, waxing the floors, dusting the furniture, washing the windows, dragging the garbage cans to the curb, negotiating with the plumber or electrician or the Roto Rooter man, cooking dinner, grocery shopping, bathing the dog, doing the taxes, and whatever else needs to be tended to nearly every single day.

Hmm...!

Maybe it wasn't just my libido I lost...maybe it was my entire mind that went AWOL.

Maybe, just maybe, when I find all my missing socks I'll find my 'mojo' again, but until that day arrives, I'll be on the search for the magic bullet.

We women know very well that menopause does strange things to our bodies, and even stranger things to our minds. We look at ourselves in the mirror and are often surprised to see that erosion is no longer just a term reserved solely for soil. All those perky parts that used to be up there have gone south and are not expected to return home any time soon, if ever!

Your nipples? Well, I have a vague memory of how proud they used to make me during the winter. You know, sweater weather nipples. They could make a grown man stop dead in his tracks. They were total boner material! Now…they sort of point towards the ground as though they're searching for missing coins.

As a matter of fact, I remember one day, a long time ago, I had to take a bus somewhere. It was summer. I was having one of those wild and free days where I decided to go braless. The bus stopped, a few people got on. This man stood in front of me and I can see him eyeballing the empty seat next to me. I couldn't figure out why he was just standing there so I say to him *sit down.* He says to me, *okay, but you're going to have to move that first!* I looked down and realized one of my girls had escaped the loose midriff top I was wearing. There wasn't really anything else I could do but reel her back in and clear the way for the guy.

I digress (again)!

What used to be my neat little waistline, well…hell! That thing now looks like a scrap yard filled with heaps of old worn out dented parts waiting to be crushed and hauled off. I never knew you could actually grow cellulite on a belly, but I was wrong. I was very wrong. My favorite trick with this newfound flesh is to squish together all the fat around my belly button to replicate the perfect bagel. I use that as a breakfast killer. Once I see *that bagel* I usually lose my appetite.

The lack of hormones, lack of energy, lack of time, lack of desire, all move us constantly towards that 'not tonight honey I've got a headache' syndrome. If that's not enough to keep him off you then you use the rubber mallet you keep on your side of the bed for just such occasions. In some cases, when his horny arrives and yours is still AWOL, it's even more drastic. It's more like 'touch me and pull back a bloody stub'. Worse yet, you can now voice the words 'touch me and die' with a single glance at your partner.

Yeah, the lost libido syndrome echoes across the nation like a sonic boom and you know who's listening to these calls for help? The pharmaceutical companies—that's who. They're very aware of the need to put the zip back in your atrophying vagina before it closes shop permanently. They know they've got you by the balls so to speak. So what do they do? They charge you a freaking arm and a leg for their products because they know that:

IF MAMA AIN'T HAPPY, NOBODY'S HAPPY!

Yep, this drug crap is expensive, and because it doesn't work like erectile dysfunction meds, which has an immediate impact, you have to take it long term to wreak any benefits.

I recently had coffee with a friend of mine and his wife. We talked about all the normal things we usually talk about, kids, life, work, whatever, but then the conversation turned to his recent bout with prostrate cancer. Now, this in itself is *not* funny at all, but his description of how his penis works now that his prostate has been removed definitely opened the door to my sick sense of humor! Not only did he have to take Viagra to get a boner, he had to give himself a shot of starch or something *right in his wiener.*

Holy crap! OMG! Jeez Louis! Arggggg!!!!!

When those words left his lips, I actually felt my vagina shrivel up into a fetal position trying to protect itself.

I'll tell you this much. If somebody told me I had to stick a needle in my vagina to achieve an orgasm, I'd likely die an old non-orgasmic spinster.

It was obvious our conversation had to be diverted at that point so I asked his wife how *her* libido was. I figured she was a safe bet to ascertain a little info on this subject because she's a little older than me. She told me that she'd had her own struggle with it over the years, having gone through menopause already, but she'd recently discovered a fantastic product that boosted her libido. She actually wanted to have sex now...with her husband!

She said it was Chinese herbs that turned it around for her. Shit! Here we go again. As much as I love the idea of natural products and herbs, I've got a cabinet full of herbal crap that promised to heal this or that with no desired results.

But, she swore by this one product (which meant one pill only), and told me I should get some for myself. I hate trying new things, especially when it comes to pills of any kind, but I was desperate. I trusted she knew what she was talking about so I let my mind do a 180-degree turn around in this case. I sucked back the rest of my coffee, excused myself, and then rushed off to the herbalist's store she'd mentioned.

I was quite shocked when I pulled into the parking lot. I was expecting to see a crappy little, dingy curtained, postage stamp size store. But no! This bloody place was the size of Costco, which meant this was going to be a time-consuming event instead of a pop in – pop out experience. But I was there and I was going to persevere for the sake of my mental health and my vagina.

Now, you have to understand, if I'd been looking

for something for a cough, or something to make me sleep, I wouldn't have hesitated to ask for help locating this particular product, but because it would be an admission of my inadequate sex drive, I cruised up and down every stinking aisle scanning bottle after bottle for what seemed like hours looking for the shiny blue bottle she'd described in detail. I couldn't find it.

I slunk up to the counter in defeat. It took the clerk a few minutes to even acknowledge my presence. When he finally looked up at me with those slanted little eyes, I couldn't tell if he was looking at me or still checking the front door to see who had come in because he had one of those *really* lazy eyes. I mean it was crazy lazy. Now, if you knew me like my pals do you'd know this about me. I can never pass up the opportunity to entertain myself, so I quietly pulled a coin out of my jeans pocket and tossed it so it landed in the first aisle about twenty feet from where I was standing. OMG! His lazy eye lit up like a candle and his head started moving as his eye tried to find the source of the noise. I can be so bad sometimes but I just can't help myself sometimes. Anyway, I finally cleared my throat to get his attention. His head swung around so fast, it took the lazy eye a moment to settle down and focus on me. I had to bite the inside of my cheek to kill the cackle trying to escape my lips, and because of all the coffee I'd just ingested an hour ago, I had to squeeze my legs together so that last cup wouldn't come gushing out of my leaky bladder. I could feel my face go from my normal pale hue to bright red as I asked him to point out the libido booster section.

"Ah Yes…Rabido…" he said looking me up and down. I saw his eyebrow go up. I knew he was judging me.

"Ah…Yeah," was about the only confirmation I could respond with.

"Rabido bloke?" he said in a half-question, half-statement tone.

I'm thinking, no asshole, I'm just here to fuck with you because that's the only kind of fucking I want to do.

"No, it's not broke! I just lost it somewhere between my forties and fifties."

"Rabido Steel…make you…hot," he says, finishing his statement by gesturing with his groin moving in that humping motion.

What? He can't see the sweat pouring down my face from the hot flash that's just ripped me a new asshole?

Holy crap. This guy suddenly looks like he's ready to go right then and there. I immediately scan his crotch in search of a spontaneous boner, but it's as flat as a pancake.

"You're sure I'm gonna wanna…" I finish by gesturing the same humping motion because at this point, I figure I've got nothing to lose here.

His eyebrows go up and down again as though he's trying to dislodge something from his forehead and he grins at me. He goes over to aisle 32, walks halfway to the back of the store, picks up a bottle, and then sets it into my sweaty palm. He seems a little reluctant to actually let it go. I try pulling it politely from his fingers but for some odd reason he's got a Chinese death grip on it. This guy's actually got the balls to try to fuck with me in this condition. Unbelievable!

How can he not know, just by looking at me, that I'm hormonally imbalanced and perfectly capable of disemboweling him with one hand tied behind my back, all in the time it would take him to take his next breath. And guess what, I'd probably get away with it in a court of law no matter whether the judge was male or female. There's an unwritten law that specifically states that when a woman hits menopause, it's like she has a restraining order against all mankind and anyone who dares to cross that hundred yards deserves whatever they get.

But no, this crazy, lazy eyed, asshole refuses to let go.

But wait!

Out of the corner of my eye I see his other hand reaching towards my right breast.

What the fuck?

My mind began to race!

Did this mean I still had it? Did he get all worked up by *my* push, push, groin thrust? Was I hot to him? Were my girls turning him on? Or did he just have a death wish?

I instantly react with the speed of a bullet leaving the barrel of a gun. I intercept his approaching paw with my best Jiu-Jitsu move and my do-jo cry– *KEYAH.*

It takes him about two seconds to turn his crazy lazy eye towards me before I can actually give him *my* evil eye glare!

He jumps back and rubs his wrist. As close together as we're standing, I can see a red welt rise where I'd just karate chopped him.

He stands there in complete shock, complete disbelief! His eyes fill with fear.

He takes a few more steps back from me then raises his shaking hand and points at my right breast.

I look down and see there is a rather large ball of white thread sticking to my black sweater. It probably came loose from the coat I'd been wearing earlier.

"Lou got shit on lour shirt rady," he says in his defense.

"Oh my god…I'm soooo sorry!" I say pulling the straggler off and tossing it to the ground.

"Maybe you need hormone too bitch...hep bain rerax," he says making his move towards the cash register.

I'm thinking this guy must be fucking telepathic because I *had* run out of estrogen. I'd been out of it, and out of my mind, for nearly a week because I'd forgotten to order it.

I try to hand him my credit card.

"No rady! No fucking way! You set card on counter, I pick up myself."

I try to gather what's left of my brain and defend my action, but the second I try to speak he shushes me.

"Shhhh...you pay me, get out," he hisses at me. "Lou no come back."

He rips my card a new asshole through his machine and tosses it back on the counter, then sets the sales slip down so I can sign it. As I reach for the pen he steps back as though he knows what my arm span is.

"Can I have a bag?"

"No, now go!" he says throwing the bottle of pills at me.

"Okie dokie then," I say reaching for my receipt. I see him jump back just far enough to stay out of harms way.

I hang my head in embarrassment and do as I'm told. As I head towards my car I can feel his eye, the crooked lazy one, burning into the back of my head. I know he's watching through the slats of the window blinds to make sure I'm really leaving and I'm pretty sure, when he see's me glance back at him, I hear the clank of a lock being engaged.

But then I thought, who cares? I'm about to get my horny on. I'm about to get my mojo back. I'm about to get myself all sexed up! I'm going to be that sexually unchallenged machine I once was. The Boner Goddess! The MILF! I may actually find that spontaneous orgasm. Wheehaw!!!!!

I get in my car and nearly have to pry my fingers off the bottle so I can read the label.

I look at the main ingredient and burst out laughing.

'Horny Goat Weed?' WTF?

It's then I realize I probably could have just as easily gone to the local feed store to get this shit.

No one's home when I get there so I crack open the bottle, tip it towards the light so I can inspect the pills inside.

You have got to be shitting me!

Say it isn't so!

Was I supposed to swallow these things, or were

they suppositories? I have panic attacks when I have to take those little Advil tablets, how was I possibly going to manage these? I look at the label and read the instructions.

Take one daily for maintenance and up to four two hours before sexual activity. I could feel the sweat breaking out on my brow.

This is ridiculous!

Now I was going to have to get anxiety medicine just to be able to swallow these suckers.

But I was on a mission. I'd just have to bite the bullet, literally, and down these Horny Goat Weed suckers any way I could.

Flash forward one week. I probably should have read the whole label so I'd be prepared for the possible side affects.

I wasn't feeling the sex thing yet, but one thing I did notice immediately was, whenever I was driving, my attention kept wandering towards the long tall grass that runs parallel to the freeway. I'd start to feel hunger pangs, followed shortly thereafter by the urge to pull over and graze on those long, lean, fluttering, nirvana inducing blades.

I even started noticing barnyard animals in the most odd places. In Los Angeles proper, it's pretty rare to see anything other than a cat or dog. But I swear I saw two goats happily grazing on a hillside not too far from my house.

I found myself wanting to visit a friend of mine's ranch up in the Santa Monica Mountains, because I'd recently attended a woman's horse retreat there and had a vague recollection of a very handsome billy goat wandering about. If I remember correctly, I think his name is Walter.

My new catch phrase became one word...Eweeeee!

I'd catch myself late at night staring down at my front lawn from my bedroom balcony.

I ordered every version of "Grazin' In The Grass Is A Gas" from iTunes.

One day my husband came home and I was laying face down in the tall cool green grass.

"What the hell are you doing?" he asked.

"Um............mowing the lawn."

"Why is your hand down your pants?"

"I got an itch." I respond.

What? Wait a minute!

Maybe it was starting to happen. Maybe it wasn't just an itch. Maybe, just maybe, my vagina was finally getting the message.

Bingo!

I looked up at him staring down at me and cocked my eyebrow.

"Kids aren't home yet. Would you like to have a staff meeting, you know, step into my barn...I mean office?"

Oh yes, the world we live in, the world I live in, is a far better place when I can chemically alter it naturally!

Sixteen

The Middle Hours...

...the ones where sleep is elusive. The ones that fall between say–two and six in the morning.

Those hours are like a secret garden for me. I plant a seed, a thought, then let the idea grow until creativity sparks like a firecracker.

Whatever happens in this time frame sets the tone for my day. It determines whether it will be a fun day or just another one of those "*funny days*!"

Why I'm up during what should be my rapid eye movement hours is beyond me...it just is what it is!

It always amazes me how we adapt and learn to tolerate that which makes us crazy, that which makes us freaking exhausted later in the day when we should be functioning like a well oiled engine!

But this time of day/night, however you want to look at it, is often my most creative time if I can harvest and hone the thoughts running through my brain…the ones that shoot out like bullets from a machine gun.

Bam–there goes another one!

Just when I think I'm coming into focus, honing in on the ramblings/ideas/thoughts scooting back and forth in my brain like a hockey puck being played by two trophy winning teams, just when I think I can sit at my computer and force words to flow through my fingers onto the blank screen, words that should make sense…

Bam, bam, bam!

I realize once again that I forgot to switch the laundry over before going to bed.

This sets off the train of frustration because I know I'll have to run the wash again to get rid of the overnight stench of sitting water. Next house, the laundry room is going be inside, not in the garage!

It's the chain reaction theory working to keep me

running behind, like a watch whose battery is on the verge of dying, but not quite. It keeps a little time, the wrong time, but it's moving just enough to keep me going even though I may reach the total fail point…the place where I give in and say time or lack of it wins–I lose.

I wonder whether or not I can achieve all the tasks ahead of me during the correct hours of being awake! Can I fit my creativity onto the list of the 'honey do' portion of my day?

WHAT'S A GIRL TO DO?

Me–I do what I always do. I step away from the computer, go out to the laundry room, set the wheels in motion once again–and feel some odd sense of satisfaction rain down in my brain.

Score Card
Chores done–10 points!
Creativity–0!
Fuck!

This happens all too often.

Returning from the laundry room, I wonder what it was that I was about to write? The idea eludes me and I feel, well, disappointed, put upon, and bummed out! Will the idea/thought return? Maybe, but maybe not!

I hate my brain some days.

But I'm a creature of habit. I force myself to sit and think.

There's an inkling of something lurking at the end of my fingertips just waiting to spring free, but the release is not there. It fades away. It's like a rain cloud that's moved in front of the sun. That's right about the time when I notice all the crap lying on the floor next to the table upon which my computer sits. This again would be due to snacks ingested by my children long after I'd hit the sack the night before.

I try to ignore the distraction by focusing on the blank screen of my computer.

One word...just type one fucking word and you can break the spell I tell myself!

I see the broom taunting me though. It always does. It's a love—hate thing. It leans against the cupboard all yellow and bristly trying so desperately to seduce me, to get and keep my attention.

"Come on...you know you want to feel my handle in your hands," it whispers into the air as though I can really hear it...as though I will really truly give a shit.

"Piss off...I'm trying to work here!" I let these words spin around in my brain silently!

"No, no, no," it whispers. "You know you can't write anything now that you've spotted the mess on the floor!"

"Shut the hell up!" This time I say it out loud, but not loud enough to wake anyone else up.

I have, on occasion, said things too-out-loud during the wee hours and as a result one of my children have wandered out of their bedroom sleepy eyed to ask me who the hell I'm talking to at this ungodly hour. That's when I have to decide between telling an outright lie, or admit that I'm having a perfectly normal conversation with the broom!

They know I talk to myself...but admitting that I have a real honest-to-God relationship with most of my cleaning utensils may lead to a lot of unsettling questions later on in life in regards to hereditary mental illness.

I try to ignore it by Googling "dealing with ADD".

Focus daily on your overall health, both in mind and body!
Don't fail to plan.
Plan to succeed!
Surround yourself with a positive environment as much as possible!

BLAH, BLAH, BLAH, BLAH, BLAH!

FOCUS...SCHMOKUS!

The authors of these great suggestions obviously do not know my family or me! They must be referring to those who are either only a tad affected by this syndrome, or are medicated so heavily they turn into iron-clad-doer's who tunnel vision everything until they've accomplished every stinking thing on their list.

My eyes are once again drawn away from the empty computer screen to those bastard crumbs!

Now, call me a freak, but this time, when I look down at them again, I see they've somehow reshaped themselves to form words:

Clean. Me. Now!

Son of a bitch!

The earth feels like it's moving beneath me. I thank God for living in California because the earth does move here. If this is an earthquake, it will relieve me of my creative duties, halleluiah, because now I'll have to run into the kitchen and try to hold as many cupboards closed as I can in order to maintain damage control.

I wait for the bigness of it.................but nothing.

I realize as my eye's turn towards the kitchen that it's just the fucking broom doing the tango because it's as ADD as me. It's demanding my attention!

At long last I close my computer in defeat!

Score Card
Chores-20 points

Creativity-0

I guess some days you've just got to go with the flow, go the way the mop flops, give in or give out, and putter rather than accomplish.

SEVENTEEN

My Boobs Have Moved South...

...for the winter or so it seems. Actually—it seems like forever at this point!

I woke up early one morning recently because my boob was suffering from a mysterious chill. I pulled the covers up but that didn't help.

That's when I realized I was sleeping on my back and my boob had fallen off the bed and was lying on the hardwood floor.

BITCH PLEASE!

I knew I should've put carpeting in the bedroom.

Accidents like this are bound to happen. I'm old enough to know better.

"What the hell girl," I said in my most scolding tone as I reeled it back on to the bed, and back under the covers where it belonged.

Thing One and Thing Two are developing a mind of their own. They have some secret agenda is what I think!

COULD THIS BE THAT PHYSICAL DISCONTENT THEY TALK ABOUT? THE ONE THAT COMES EVERY WINTER...THE ONE THAT COMES AS EACH DECADE PASSES?

Are our bodies searching to redefine how it will appear to the general public right now? Is this what happens, in the way of consequences, as we slack off on our maintenance of it?

Or was Thing One actually searching for something in the form of that warm ray of sunshine that was lurking just beyond the curtains as the sun began to rise?

Both of those little buggers should be satisfied

with the heat brought on by those bloody hot flashes that course through my aging body at a surprising rate of speed, wherever and whenever they feel like showing up.

Or could it be I've reach the time in my life, once again, where a sleeping bra would make sense? I wore one during my pregnancies to keep the girls closer to home when all they wanted to do was play.

Oh yes! That was very interesting.

The word 'undulation' is what comes to mind when I think of how they used to misbehave back then. Their favorite game was to imitate a yo-yo when I moved about.

Bada-boing, bada-boing, bada-boing!

Up down, up down, and sometimes even, as an added treat, a loop de loop.

As a matter of fact, my boobs were so out of control when I was breast feeding my babies in the morning, I could actually do it without any physical contact. Thing One and Thing Two would be so swollen with milk upon waking that, if I heard them cry, my milk would shoot out like that *fill the clowns mouth and break the balloon* game you see at all the carnivals. All I had to do is teach them to keep their mouths open and they would never go hungry.

Yes, my boobs have a secret life of their own.

They're always looking for attention—good, bad, or indifferent!

I recall another occasion a few years back when I was rudely awakened in the wee hours of the morning because I couldn't breathe.

What the hell? What on earth was happening?

The first thought that came to mind was that hubby had finally had enough of my crazy antics and was trying to off me. He sometimes has these little adventures in his sleep, which I think make's him far crazier than me.

Oops! Did I say that out loud? Sorry honey, but in my defense–you do have those wacky dreams that set you out on a mission of sorts.

My bad!

When my eyes popped open–an auto-reflex due to lack of oxygen–I could see he was still sound asleep and facing in the other direction. He was off the hook.

I reached up towards my throat and that's when I discovered that Thing Two had decided to sleep in the crook of my neck.

Little bitch! I take very good care of the girls so this kind of behavior is shocking!

Were my boobs screaming out for security once again?

Hmm…?

Or was it just a matter of weight distribution? Could it be the extra weight I'd recently acquired had chosen to settle in my boobs as it often does?

Anyone out there with large boobs knows that this is only a few of the pitfalls of large mammary glands.

Life's a bitch sometimes!

Maybe this is yet another reason to keep duct tape in the drawer next to my bed!

EIGHTEEN

Dear Thing One And Thing Two...

...please accept my apologies for anything you may have overheard during that heated conversation I was having with myself the other day when you were misbehaving.

You know that I have these random 'talks' with myself, so I don't know why you were so shocked, and I don't quite understand why you reacted so irrationally. You should be used to that by now. I expected better of you!

Jacqui Brown

I just wanted to remind you that it's been a lot of fun hanging with you all these years. We've traveled, reveled, placated, and well, we've done a lot. I know at times it's been tough and I know you hate those nasty exams, but hey, it's for your own good. I wish you wouldn't complain so often because I'm only doing what I'm told to do in order to keep you healthy.

That being said, I have to say I was pretty mad at you for moving without telling me first, but I'm over that now. As a landlord, I've never liked lease breakers, but I'm willing to look the other way at least for the moment.

You've both been faithful friends throughout my life and I know you've had to bounce around a lot! My apologies! Had I known that this bothered you so much I may have found a way to be more uplifting, more supportive. I would have shopped at Victoria's Secret instead of Target.

Even though your perkiness has slowly been diminishing over the past couple of years I can't help thinking that you threw in the towel a little early in the game.

I will miss seeing you on a day-to-day basis.

Love, Mom

~///~

Dear Mom,

Thanks for the note.

We always love to hear you blather about how much you love us.

We too were sorry we had to vacate the premises, but it was becoming, without a doubt, very obvious that moving south was our only option.

We have, and will always regard your chest as our first and favorite home, but here's the deal.

We're tired of always having to act as your frontmen. Yes, we were able to get you into certain places because of our good looks, and yes we could always help you win over strangers by pointing out just how lovely you are, but the reality is, you've squeezed out about all you're going to get from us without some kind of compensation.

Unfortunately, we also felt incredibly let down on occasion, so we felt we had to take it upon ourselves to relocate to a friendlier, less obtrusive location.

Please refer to our bulleted note.

Below is our list of complaints:

* We were tired of being gawked at over the years

and never listened to.

* We were, on many occasions, forced to hold our breath because your clothes were too small, too tight, or both. There were a few close calls when we thought the damage would be permanent!

* We grew weary of catching crumbs during mealtimes. You have no idea how harsh a little piece of granola can be when it's hot and humid!

* We resent the fact that your exercise routine did not include us as much as we needed to be included, thus, it's your own fault we were forced to join a swingers club.

WE ARE SHY CREATURES AND THIS IS NOT FUN!

Rest assured we are happy, warm, and feel very secure in our new home.

So as not to add injury to insult, please make sure you do not put anything sharp in the front pockets of your pants so we do not suffer any undue injuries.

Thank you,

Thing One and Thing Two.

~///~

Dear T One and Two,

I shall take into consideration all your stated grievances however, since you no longer will be habitating the area between my face and my belly button, I have been forced to sign a new lease for your old location.

The new tenant, Ms. Double Chin, will take up residence as soon as possible. This is a move that both she and I have been anticipating for some time now.

This will require some alterations that may affect you but should not add to your aggravation.

Think of her as a welcome guest.

To make Ms. Chin feel safe and secure, it will be necessary to add a third cup to all your currents togs. I will do my best to color coordinate all materials, keeping in mind that you love luxury.

See you around, Mom

~///~

Dear Landlord,

We object to this intrusion!

Two's company...three's a crowd.

Fuck you!!

Don't you ever listen to your own advice?

Please stop writing to us as we can no longer respond to your demands! This is a direct quote from T One by the way, who says she no longer wants to speak to you.

Ms. Chin, to whom we have always looked up to, only adds insult to injury, especially now that she's honing in on our old stomping grounds. We will try not to hold a grudge against her, because really, this is all your fault!

Remember, we still have one other location to consider and will not hesitate to go there. As much as we would prefer to stay where we are, Sockville is still an option. We can make your life extremely uncomfortable so please, consider carefully any further decisions that would force our hand.

T One and T Two

~///~

To whom it may concern,

Do not threaten me!

Your mother.

PS: Do I have to remind you that it's summer and I won't be wearing socks very often? If you don't watch your step you could end up homeless! How embarrassing that will be for you!

Nineteen

Sexual Napalm...

...is the latest catch phrase according to a new report.

Leave it to the GenX crowd to come up with that one. Obviously they have yet to be medicated, and secondly, they haven't got a bloody clue about life yet.

Guys revealing their inner most desires when it comes to what turns them on is nothing new.

Selfish bastards!

They say they like girls who go down on them because that doesn't happen that often...

Excuse me while I puke?

Hello!

I call bullshit on this one! Just ask the hubby!

In my limited experience with dating, the first thing out of a guy's mouth was definitely not my 'vagina'.

Maybe I missed the class in semaphore they offered in high school that said—*go here not there!*

Another biggie that came to 'light' in this report is that guys like girls who like having sex with the lights on. Some even said they'd like to do it under a spotlight so they could see every inch of whom they were about to do.

At my age...*I DON'T THINK SO MUCHACHO!*

Not only would this make me uncomfortable, I don't know that I could suck my stomach in that long. My biggest complaint is that this 'revelation time' could add an extra hour to what should take less than ten minutes. I need my sleep, remember? I am early to bed, early to rise. The last thing on my mind is to add more time than necessary to this event.

Romantic Interlude Under The Spotlight

ME: "Are you done yet?"

HUBBY: "I think you're going to have to roll over one more time. I think I missed a spot. Oh wait, before you roll over can you move the light closer?"

ME: "Why is this taking so long? Are you fucking blind?"

HUBBY: "I didn't know it was going to take this long, okay?"

ME: "What are you saying?"

HUBBY: "Ah...absolutely nothing!"

I BEGRUDGINGLY ROLL OVER.

HUBBY: "Hmm...!"

ME: "What?"

HUBBY: "Nothing!"

ME: "Then what was the hmm for?"

HUBBY: "Do you want to walk in the morning?"

ME: "What?......Why do you ask?"

HUBBY: "I don't know, just thought we could use some exercise."

ME: "Bastard!"

HUBBY: "What, I'm just sayin..."

ME: "I've got a suggestion too! Why don't you just roll over and get some sleep."

HUBBY: "But?"

ME: "Nite, nite!"

SPOTLIGHT...MY ASS!

If hubby had to take that extra time to scan every part of me, we'd probably end up not having sex. With two kids still living at home our time's limited to stolen moments so there will never be a spotlight in the bedroom. Besides that, I don't want to always wonder whether this is another one of those obvious un-obvious fat checks?

At this juncture of my life, the words 'sexual napalm' bring to mind my ever constant problem...my mid-life gas tank.

Now there's sexual napalm I can relate to.

I've learned over the years to keep a spare pack of

GasX in my bedside table in case I see that glint in hubby's eyes. There's a lot of things we let slide in our long time marriage, but the passing of gas during a romantic interlude is not something we can let go. Literally! There has to be rules and this falls into the top heap.

We've tried to up our sexual napalm. This theory has been tested here and there, when on rare occasion we'd pull out *the book* and try on a few Karma Sutra positions. Most of the time I'd just stare at the pictures completely dumbfounded. I'd sit there wondering whether if, even in my twenties, I could ever accomplish some of these positions!

This is where you double up on the GasX!

I know last time we tried one of those convoluted twisted up, twirling, crazy ass positions it wasn't exactly what I'd call fun. Shortly after the paramedics left claiming that our dilemma did not constitute what they'd call an actual emergency...I put that book away.

If I want to look that ridiculous, I'll just dust off our twister game so everyone can laugh their ass off!

I'll tell you what sexual napalm is.

It's when your guy takes out the garbage without you having to ask ten times. It's when they don't drop their clothes on the floor in their normal heap because they know you'll go into maid mode as soon as you get out of bed. It's when they look at you '*that*' way instead of '*THAT*' way, you know, when you're forced to wonder if there's something wrong with your hair, makeup, clothes, or size. It's when they hold your hand when you least expect it. It's when, on occasion, they hold their tongue when they see you bathed in sweat for no obvious reason.

But most of all, it's when they respond to you, no matter what's going on, with the perfect phrase:

'Honey, let me get you a glass of wine!'

wenty

Dear Ms. Le. Bido...

...I know you've had a lot on your mind over the years but I wanted you to know that I miss you terribly.

OH MY FUCKING GOD DO I MISS YOU!

Oh and yes, if you're wondering, Mr. Dick Wad misses you as well!

I know that for a long time you've been down in

the dumps and tossed around like a cheap salad because I've been so busy with my life, but I just don't understand why you're not responding to any of my e-mails or calls?

I don't remember abusing you or misusing you in any way, so I just don't get it!

I've been searching for you non-stop these past few years.

I've looked under the couch hoping maybe you'd somehow accidentally slipped out that night I had one to many tequila's and slept with my legs askew. That would have been an easy fix since I could have just slipped you back inside and no one would have been the wiser.

But no, you were nowhere to be found!

I've looked in the back of my closet and inside all my boots thinking maybe you felt you needed a break and quietly slid down my leg that day I had to stand in line at Costco while forty-two thousand people checked out in front of me.

I have this vague memory of a horrible itch that day. I seem to recall it was really hot and my panties were making me uncomfortable, but it would have been too embarrassing to scratch 'down there' in public. I'm sorry if that made you uncomfortable, so again I apologize if you felt neglected.

I've searched and searched endlessly!

Hell, I've even scoured my underwear drawer several times, hoping that perhaps you just got stuck on one of my thongs, but my search proved fruitless, although I did actually find a few other things that have been missing for awhile.

No. You have simply vanished!

I recently put up posters hoping that someone would recognize you and bring you home safe and sound, but apparently posting pictures of an atrophied vagina, even as a most wanted poster, is against the law here. Something to do with porn and privacy laws.

I found this out the hard way after two uniformed officers showed up at my house informing me that in order for me to continue putting up these posters I would have to add a pair of underwear to the picture to cover Ms. Gina, and I wasn't sure, since you've been gone so long, which underwear you would recognize.

It's been a tough road without you, and although it's far more work these days to get my mojo on, I persevere.

I'm still holding out hope that one of these days we'll cross paths again.

Until we meet again,

Mom

~///~

Dear Mom,

Whaa, whaa, whaa!

Here's the deal. You're very needy. I had to make a stand. My biggest beef is that I felt over worked and underpaid.

Sex, sex, and more sex! Whoo hoo for you!

Jeez Louis!

You never gave me a break so I did what I had to do. I slipped out the back door during one of your, ahem, midnight silent killers.

I knew this would be the only way I could make a clean exit. Well actually, I guess it wasn't exactly clean in that sense, but your hubby was so busy trying to get the pillow over his head I knew you wouldn't even notice I was gone until it was too late to do anything about it.

Just to let you know, I plan on coming back some day, but it's not going to happen any time soon. I need more time. I need to nurture myself a little. You've worked me hard for the last 35 years or so. I think I deserve some time off for good behavior. Besides, when you break a sweat, do you think it's any fun for me being stuck in your latest of trendy underwear? I don't think so!

I know you've been trying to lure me back and I'm absolutely appalled at the depths to which you can sink.

That horny goat weed shit was child's play. You actually thought you could drug me into returning?

Oh, and by the way, I'm currently in rehab thank you very much!

You're such a fool.

If you were serious about trying to get me back you might want to step on the treadmill once in a while. I hear exercise really helps.

And while we're on the subject, perhaps you'll consider one less shot of tequila at night. This fucks with your brain as well as mine.

These are not threats but I want you to take me seriously!

I know what you said to Thing One and Two and you just don't scare me anymore. One and Two still speak to me and they agree with the exercise thing.

Yours truly,

Ms. Le. Bido

~///~

Dearest Bashing Bido,

You suck!

Please do not rush back for my sake...BITCH!

You should know better than to bite the hand that feeds you!

Up yours,

You know who!

Twenty - One

Feng Shui-ing My Body...

...in order to have a better mental image of myself has been one bloody, difficult task.

Although no people or animals were hurt in the process of this time sensitive endeavor, several mirrors in my home were destroyed. Three spontaneously combusted, the other two wouldn't so I had to take matters into my own hands.

When 'Feng meets Shui' (this happens a lot if you walk too fast) you are in essence, supposed to be in tune with yourself.

OH WHATEVER!

Finding what that tune is when your mind is wandering through the abyss of menopause, is almost impossible!

Tuning in means you're supposedly supposed to be in a place where you're in spiritual, emotional, and physical alignment, therefore, the need for reflection should only take place in one's mind.

Wish I'd realized this before I destroyed every reflective surface in my house! It's rather difficult to put makeup on by memory.

This tuning in crap, I mean-process, will likely put you in a bad mood because, what you're about to discover is this:

...your brain has become this God-awful emotional dumping ground, and you're gonna have to buck up or shut up!

Spring-cleaning is imminent and essential if you're going to go down this road!

Great. That's one more chore! Just what we need, right?

In order to get the process going, you're gonna need a vacuum with turbo power and a tiny hose attachment, organic spray cleaner, and a scrub brush to rid your mind of some of the more clingy shit.

If you're still raising children, well, good luck with the clingy shit!

Worst case scenario, you'll need a good mind altering medication prescribed from your, ahem, 'medical marijuana doctor'.

So, that being said, let's get down to the nitty of the gritty!

Many of us mid-lifers have acquired more Shui than Feng. You know, like when your ass has to catch up with the rest of your body whenever you're moving. This is especially evident when it's time to change the clocks in the spring. While the rest of me 'springs forward, my butt stays an hour behind!"

Wearing crystals on our body seems like an uncomfortable solution, but deep down, I feel like this could be the solution we've been looking for.

I've been searching the ends of the earth trying to find 'said crystals' that are flat and unobtrusive, because the last thing we need is more protrusions, right?

I've yet to be successful because so far, the ones I have found and tried to utilize have these sharp little edges that make me itch. If you're a Spanx lover, well, the annoying factor doubles.

That's not the only problem either! Because I'm

more the fitted clothing kind of gal, these 'said crystals' also cause some pretty wacky protrusions that become very obvious under your clothing. If positioned incorrectly, you'll have lumps and bumps (the exact opposite of what you're trying to go for) in places that will make people give you odd glances.

I've tried putting them in obvious places in order to draw attention away from places I don't want people gawking at, but this only irritated 'THING ONE' and 'THING TWO'.

Maybe now that it's winter, you know, sweater weather, this will finally work in my favor!

The hubby's a little freaked by this whole idea.

After running his hand down my back towards my butt the other day, he accidentally came across one of my lovely hidden gems. He asked me why I was going to such extremes with this insanity?

"Honey, I'm trying to clean up my temple! I'm trying to draw good things to all parts of my body," I say.

"I've got a good thing for your body right here, in my pocket, and it's free!" he says, hoping as always, that I'll jump at the opportunity to allow him to help me in my quest for peace.

My idea of 'HAVING PEACE' is far different from his idea of 'HAVING A PIECE'.

"Look. I need to figure out my ba-gua, my energy map," I tell him. "I need to figure out how I can use my body to increase my income potential."

DEAD SILENCE!

I look at him and he's smiling.

"If you put all your energy into my ba-gua for five minutes, I think I've got some cash in my wallet," he says.

MEN!

At first, I was insulted by his 'cash for gash' comment, but the more I thought about it, I realized he might have a point.

The 'law of Feng Shui' says that to attract more prosperity into your life, you should include wood and water. Somewhere in the back of my mind, I recall one of my daughter's old boyfriends who, when horny, used to tell her, "I GOT WOOD!" He'd see a cool car and he'd say, 'MAN THAT GIVES ME WOOD'. HE'D SEE A PRETTY GIRL...AHHH....WOOD BABY, WOOD!

I'd already done my research. I knew my personal element was fire.

Hmm...

Fire requires a lot of wood...

INTERESTING!

Maybe hubby's not such a pig after all. Maybe he's been doing his own research. Maybe he's been looking through my notes. Maybe, just maybe, he's about to get lucky. This could become one of those rare 'win-win' situations we love so much.

"HONEY?" I SAY, LOOKING HIM SQUARE IN THE EYE.

"Yes?" he says.

And yes, I can still hear the tiniest amount of hope in his voice.

"Exactly how much cash do you have in your wallet?"

Twenty - Two

Dry Skin Versus Oily Skin...

...is another thing we menopausal women have to deal with.

I for one am of the dry skin group. Just my luck, right?

I've become the fucking Sahara Desert inside and out.

If I manage to drool at night, I don't get upset. No way!

I become elated, overjoyed, wrought with happiness, because that means my body went into overdrive during the night just to produce that one little droplet of moisture. It's a sign from God that there's still hope that one day my moisture will return!

If I spit when I talk, I thank God!

I scream halle-fuckin-lulia at the top of my lungs because it's possibly going to be one of those glorious days where my tongue's not stuck to the roof of my mouth or the back of my teeth.

Yep! I'm like a long hot summer day. *Dry with no chance of rain!*

When hubby get's that look in his eye, you know, where he's staring at my vagina, I have to remind him that:

"Just because something looks like an oasis–it doesn't always mean it is an oasis!"

A friend of mine always complains about how oily her skin has gotten since she hit menopause.

If that were me, and that oil made its way to my vagina, I'd get down on my fucking knees and praise God!

This of course is all good news for the pharmaceutical companies though. Now they can expand their profits by developing new products like 'Gina Juice'!

There's already a plethora of new products out there for those of us who are atrophying, drying up like prunes as we venture through this wonderful phase we loving call menopause.

I tried one of those new 'hot lubricants' a few weeks back. Let me tell you!

I can now officially say that I smoke after sex.

Hubby: "You smoking in bed?"

Me: "No!"

Hubby: "I smell smoke."

Me: "I'm not smoking, dammit!"

Hubby: "Somebody's smoking!"

Me: "No one is smok…"

Of course, that's when I realize something's going on down there. My vagina has become some kind of heat seeking vessel and she's burning up.

Crap!

I peek under the sheet and sure as hell, there it is. There's a cloud of smoke! I realize immediately that if I lay there, there's a good chance I'll set the sheets on fire.

So much for that lingering about after hot sex!

I jump out of bed and head for the shower. Now there's no hiding the fact that I'm hot. I'm surrounded in smoke and the faster I move, the bigger the cloud gets. Hubby notices right away.

Hubby: "Wow, you are hot!"

Me: "Don't ever forget it!"

Twenty - Three

Marriage Can...

...definitely take a bite out of your freedom, that's for damn sure. But I like it.

I've been in the business for more than thirty years so I guess it's safe to say, it kind of suits me to a 'T'.

I find great comfort in knowing that, when I walk back into my house at the end of the day, there's more than just the dog there waiting to stick his wet muzzle up into my butt crack just so he can relay his feelings of:

'Mommy, you're home! I missed you! Where the hell have you been all day? Can I have a treat? Where's my dinner? Rub my belly! Can we go for a walk?'

Not that a simple kiss on the cheek wouldn't do the same thing.

It may seem like a cheap thrill, and it is, but I'm easy. I'll take them whenever I can! Time passes too quickly and cheap thrills don't arrive on your doorstep all that often!

Yes, this is my dog's favorite thing to do. On a good day he'll nudge me this way from the front door all the way into the kitchen.

Don't get me wrong here. I appreciate the fact that he likes my ass just as much as the hubby does.

Now, whether it's that his nose is itchy, as it always is, or whether this is truly a sign of love, I don't mind so much because I know he needs me, he cherishes our time together, and he can't stand it when I'm gone too long.

Again, this is where the hubby and dog are similar!

Hubby also likes to push his nose into the crack of my butt, misses me when I'm gone, wants a snack, wonders where dinner is, loves to have his belly rubbed, then wants me to walk around the block with him.

Only difference here is that I don't have to carry a crap bag, although there's always a certain amount of bullshit I have to put up with, but I don't have to wipe the drool off...

Oh...wait...that's wrong because sometimes I do. Sigh!

Yes, this is where two great minds work like one great machine!

Over the years, I've come to the understanding that husbands are a lot like dogs. Their bark is usually worse than their bite. It's usually only a slight flesh wound if they do in fact decide to take a chomp out of you, because guess what? They're not going to do anything that would jeopardize their butt-sniffing privileges.

They can be:

...mischievous

...patient

...impatient

...loving

...generous

...jealous

...as well as a plethora of other emotions.

Husbands master the art of 'puppy dog eyes' better than some dogs sometimes, especially when it comes to sex.

They'll gladly roll over so you can rub their belly and whatever else is in the region. Usually this is where the wagging tail comes in.

If you use your wily womanly ways in just the right way they're also easily trainable. You can bet your bottom dollar on that!

You throw them a bone and you can be damn sure they're going to sit up and beg until that bone is secured tightly in their teeth. Or in hubby's case, until the boner...I mean bone... is securely in your teeth!

Mornings are especially interesting at my house. We have this routine you see. It's not always exactly the same but for the most part it's our thing. It's been happening for years and years.

I get up in the middle of the night in order to have some peaceful, quite, writing time. This is what I tell myself anyway, but of course I know the truth. It all boils down to menopausal instability, which includes those fantastic hot flashes, the inability to turn my brain off, and the sudden penchant for undisturbed housecleaning.

It's exactly the time when I think of all the things I

don't want to think about.

If I slept longer than three o'clock in the morning, I'd have to do a pulse check. I've made peace with this over the years because I don't have a choice. It's really not so bad, except that I can no longer stay up later than nine p.m. Some say this makes me boring.

I say to those people—Piss off!

In the middle of the night the world is peaceful.

The kids are snug in their beds.

The dog's rolled over on his back on the couch in the den, his legs moving as thought he's chasing someone or something, and hubby, well, he's lost in dreams with a big old smile on his face. Obviously he's dreaming about me!

The best part of the early morning for me happens after the coffee's brewed. I've got my electric blanket cranked to high. It always seems to be cold in my office so my son thought this would be a brilliant Christmas gift a year ago. What a thoughtful boy. I love it, I use it, and it serves its purpose wonderfully. I've discovered however, that if you sit on electric blanket long enough, you'll actually put your vagina to sleep.

First time that happened I thought my horny had finally emerged, but upon standing, it was soon apparent that there was no feeling whatsoever, nada, nothing. Not even that pins and needles sensation. I tried touching it once just to make sure it was still there, and even that gave me no sensation. I no longer sit on the blanket. This is not a cheap thrill moment! *This* is moving in exactly the direction I'm trying to avoid.

I have enough trouble pumping that sucker up to the point where it wants to see a little action, so putting it to sleep is the last thing in the world I'd do *on purpose*!

So, somewhere around seven in the morning I hear this warbled voice barreling down the staircase. It's a cry for coffee. Yes, I'm a sucker (or maybe I'm the well-trained puppy). I stop what I'm doing and go to make his morning java.

So here comes the habit thing...

As I go up the stairs, I either hear the television or I don't.

If I hear it that means that there'll be no booty call. If I don't hear it, well, that's a whole different ball game.

That signifies it's game on.

If this is the case, then I must decide on whether or not there will be a random grab from my underwear drawer.

Oh! To lingerie or not to lingerie, that is the

question!

This is always a stab in the dark, especially if this occurs before the sun's up. I keep my panties and bra's in the same drawer. If you've ever made the mistake of trying to put a bra on in place of your underwear, well, 'Ms. Gina' will end up looking a little like an Eskimo girl, sporting an afro and lovely lacy earmuffs. It doesn't happen often, but it has.

Losing momentum sucks as far as I'm concerned!

I guess at this point in our lives we have to seize the moment at every given moment, right?

That's hubby's theory.

Actually, now that I think about it he's always ready, willing, and able.

But, it has to be quick. I've got two kids to get out the door so speed is important.

This is where all those Evelyn Wood speed classes I took years ago come in handy.

Twenty - Four

Leg Cramps...

...are more a pain in the ass than they are in the leg.

Actually, it's not necessarily the pain that concerns me; it's more the fact that it turns me into a complete spasmodic imbecile in the middle of the night.

I'm glad to know though, that I'm not suffering alone!

I had lunch with a friend recently and during the course of our conversation, I discovered that she too suffers from this odd malady as well.

Misery loves company right?

We ran through the age appropriate symptoms we're prone to, saggy neck, saggy boobs, saggy butt, but we kept coming back to those damned leg cramps.

"Sometimes my leg takes on a life of its own in the middle of the night," she says.

"Sometimes my leg takes on a life of its own in the middle of the night and then it starts beating up my other well-behaved leg," I say.

"Sometimes my leg takes on a life of its own and I 'use' my other leg to beat the misbehavior into submission," she says.

"Sometimes my leg takes on a life of its own…" I say pausing to catch my breath. "Oh hell girl, we're just getting old."

"Your are–I'm not," she says.

"Are too! You're older than me," I say in defense of my three months younger than her youthfulness.

"By what, one fucking hair?" she retorts.

As always, my hand flies up to my chin and sure enough–there it is!

That was what I was trying to remember all morning. I was supposed to get my tweezers back from little Miss Esthetician so I could remove the scraggly little unkempt hair that's decided to take up residence on my chin. Damned her to hell! She's going to pay for my friends remark when I get home.

"Are you inferring that I'm old?" I shoot back.

"No. Just that I'm older by a smidgen," she says.

"Oh I see. We're going to go there are we?"

She raises her eyebrow in answer.

"Maybe," she says.

"Well, if you want to "string" this along," I say, my smile broadening as I run my fingers through my thick dark hair.

She's blonde and thinning. I know this will leave a scar.

She immediately goes into her Jaclyn Smith/Charlie's Angels hair toss to fluff up her bangs. It's always the same. Run the fingers through the hair to separate the strands so she can create the illusion of body. This is usually followed immediately by another shake of the head so everything falls into place.

"Speaking of smidgen, how's the diet going?" she says breaking off a morsel of the stupid ass little piece of salmon that's lying on top of the fucking lettuce on her plate.

My fork stops midway to my mouth.

Oh Bitch Please!

It's pretty obvious my hand got the message, but my mouth must have missed it because it remained open awaiting the food. She knows I've been trying to drop twenty pounds.

I look at the huge twirl of pasta on my fork. I know there's enough on it for two bites. For one brief moment I consider dropping the fork back on to my plate feigning 'I'm done', but wait–I'm still starving. And I still want to finish that slice of warm French bread that I, only moments ago, slathered with butter.

I can't really do numbers in my head but rough calculations estimate there's at least 380 calories currently on my fork.

I look at the plate.

Crap!

She might have me on this one!

My internal dialogue is rummaging around at the speed of light looking for a good comeback, something snide, yet witty.

I got nothing.

Big fucking blank!

My hand goes on autopilot and stuffs the pasta in my mouth.

"So…! What *do you* take for the leg cramps?" I ask.

Twenty - Five

New Unemployment Statistics...

...are proof that unemployment is still vastly out of control.

Duh!

Looking for work is my new full-time job!

If they could make this a paying position, I'd be stinking rich right now.

Hubby asked me the other day, "What kind of jobs are you looking for?"

"Oh, I don't know. I suppose at this point I'll take just about anything." I say flippantly.

He doesn't move away, which causes me to lose focus on the computer.

I look up at him standing there square in front of me. I see the gleam in his eye.

He's so transparent.

"Well, when you're done on the computer, *I've* got a job for you," he offers, as though I didn't know that was coming.

I try to look all shy and shit, but he waits for it. He knows me better than that!

"Asshole!" This is my standard reply after all these years together. "Get in line buddy!" I say, confident that this will, okay maybe not absolutely, positively, make him pause and wonder what I actually do when I leave the house, then come home still unemployed.

I know I'm a great asset to any company. Or maybe, it's just that I have a reasonably great ass that any company would want to have around.

I've had exactly...

Okay. So. No. One. Else. has offered this type of employment in a while, but I sure as hell am not going to let him think that he's the *only* recruiter that's checked out my resume or credentials.

Fuck that!

After 33 years of marriage, you've got to work a lot harder at making the spouse jealous, but I consistently try. It keeps things interesting!

An hour later, I close the computer. I'm frustrated!

I want a job!

Any job!

I go upstairs only to discover he's in the shower.

I see his pants on the floor.

Hmm…

I rustle through his pockets and find his wallet.

Interesting.

Jackpot!

Seems he's freakin' loaded today.

Perhaps a little part time job at this moment won't be so bad after all.

I pocket a $100 bill.

I get undressed, and then join him in the shower.

I try to look business like!

"Coming to apply for the job?" he says with that come-hither look spread across his face.

"Will there be overtime?"

"With any luck," he says. "With any luck!"

$\mathcal{T}$wenty - $\mathcal{S}$ix

$\mathcal{T}$he $\mathcal{R}$ooter $\mathcal{M}$an...

...informed me the other day that my *'flange'* was too high.

Excuse me?

No one's ever been brave enough to point that flaw out to me before, not even the hubby, at least not right to my face, and never out loud!

I have to admit I was a little shocked that it was

the second thing out of his mouth right after, "I'm the rooter guy, ma'am".

Ma'am?

Son of a bitch!

Believe me, I've had plenty of experience with inflammatory remarks before, mainly because I have kids, but my *'flange'* for God's sakes?

This was far and beyond any insult I've ever had to deal with.

I excused myself and went to do a mirror check.

Certainly my flange could not be the girls since they've relocated all on their own, and they certainly have not moved upwards (except when I pile them into my new sexy Victoria's Secret bra!) Besides that, he said 'flange' not 'flange's'. He was obviously pointing out something in the 'singular'.

My butt? Hmm…

Now, if he was referring to my butt that would actually be a good thing. It would mean all those hard 'ass' moves I've taken on at the gym were finally beginning to pay off.

But then I saw it, that little fudge-pudge that likes to hang over the top of my pants.

Oh Lord!

Was he referring to my muffin top? That's singular *and* all encompassing.

Perhaps this is why nothing really fits anymore.

Once your flange has been flagged I guess there's no going back!

I decided to change my top before returning back to where *Mr. Big Mouth* Rooter Man was working. Big and baggy would now rule the day.

Upon my return, he glanced up and his expression changed from what had been moderately happy, to something more in the confused category. More like, 'I was enjoying the view of your cleavage and now I can't see anything' kind of disappointed look.

"I liked the other top better," he said as he pulled more snake out of his rooter machine.

"Oh, I, well...I spilled something on it so I changed," I shot back.

"Just sayin'...the tighter one suits you better!" he says. "I'm just about done here. I cut the flange down so it's lower and the toilet will sit properly now."

"Oh?" I say.

"Yeah, the flange has to be set firmly against the concrete, otherwise your toilet will always leak. It's good now. Shouldn't leak any more."

Oh my little mind!

Why, oh, why, do you always have to go there? Always racing around in such an unpredictable way?

After he left I closed the gate at the end of the driveway. I stood there and watched his truck disappear into the mid-morning traffic.

This was my moment!

I could finally let out my stomach!

Other than hitting the gym every day, this is the only time these muscles get a workout!

Just as I was about to go inside the house though, my gardener pulled up.

Once again I open the gate.

He came in, looked me up and down for a moment.

First thing out of his mouth, "Mrs. Brown, your weeds are too high!"

Crap!

I immediately pulled my baggy shirt down to cover my crotch.

What is with these guys?

I excused myself, went inside the house, pulled my

pants down, inspected my groin, then picked up the phone and booked yet another Brazilian!

Sheesh! The things we do for beauty, ego, or to save ourselves from useless embarrassment!

EPILOGUE

I'll keep this short and sweet.

NEVER, UNDER ANY CIRCUMSTANCES, MESS WITH A MENOPAUSAL WOMAN!

COMING SOON

BITCH PLEASE!
VOLUME II

Getting Older...

...sucks sometimes.

Actually–it sucks all the time, right?

Now I'm not talking about your everyday normal stuff like wrinkles or saggy skin, although those two particular things make me want to destroy every reflective surface on earth. We already know those things are going to atrophy as we age. They're predictable and inevitable.

What I'm talking about is when your body starts altering itself—all by itself!

Here's my latest problem:

My damn hip tends to crack a lot, as does my back, especially during sex. So, after much deliberation, I decided to bite the bullet and head off to see the chiropractor.

Now, I'm one of those people who hates to waste time, so I usually try to book the first appointment of the day. Easy in, easy out!

At 8:45 a.m. I pull into the parking lot behind the doctor's office. At 8:52 a.m. I walk in the door, I sign in, then take the clipboard with the forms I'm asked to fill out. By 8:56 a.m. I return the clipboard to the lovely receptionist. She flips the page checking my cognitive prowess, and then asks me to follow her.

She leads me into an exam room, and then tells me the 'doctor' will be in shortly. So far, so good!

I sit down as directed and wait.

Then I wait, and wait, and wait some more.

This is bullshit because, not only is the doctor late, I'm now stuck in this crappy, dreary 5 X 5 room, with nothing more to read than National Geographic magazines from the 1970's.

Rule #1: All medical offices should be required by the law of etiquette to provide current reading material…or be on fucking time!

Thirty minutes later the doctor walks in with my chart in his hands.

"Good morning Mrs. Brown," he says.

Well, YE-FUCKIN'-HAW, I think to myself.

My time is apparently not as important as his time. We'll see about that!

"Mrs. Brown?" he says again trying to get my attention.

I decide to ignore him and continue reading the story on why Orangutans asses are so red because we should all know the answer to this age-old question.

He clears his throat several times trying to get my attention.

"I should be done here in about 27 minutes," I say checking my watch. "Why don't you just have a seat doc. I'll be right with you."

"I'm sorry I'm so late. I had an emergency," he says.

Yeah. I can see the emergency because he forgot to wipe the fucking cream cheese off the side of his face! Asshole!

I finally acquiesce and put the magazine down.

"So. What is it you're doing when your hip and back crack?" he asks.

I unbutton my pants and lower my zipper a few inches…

"What the hell are you doing?" he stammers as though he's about to choke on his own words.

"Hey…you asked me what I was doing when my hip cracked, right? Just give me a second," I say defending my actions.

"Wait just a damned a minute, let me get a nurse in here," he says, as his face turns a gentle shade of red. He slams his hand onto the button next to the door. Without missing a beat, he slides along the wall until he reaches the box of latex gloves, grabs a couple, retreats back to his spot by the door, then quickly dons said gloves.

I do not share with him that I'm only unbuttoning my pants because I've got one of those rip roaring errant gas bubble's jetting around in my gut. You know the kind. It the one that settles right at the waistband of your pants and you need to relieve the pressure by any means possible or else that suckers gonna blow right then and there. It's probably because I got up too early, drank far too much coffee that morning, and the shit, shower, and shave was not a fate-accomplis.

Regardless…I wait for his partner in crime.

I have to say this much though, I'm a little creeped out that he thinks I'd go there…with him! Hello!

If I were going for that, I'd have chosen a much younger and much better looking doctor. Perhaps even one that was more gynecologically adept. Maybe even someone who had a little

Chippendales experience under his belt.
This guy…NOT SO MUCH!
Whatever!

A few minutes later…enter *Nurse Ratchet*.

HOLY CRAP!

This nurse is like a wall-sized condom. Talk about your protective barrier! Sheesh! This gal's ankles have to be at least a size 22, and by the size of her bicep's, it's pretty apparent that she's a definite gym rat.

She looks at me then back at the doctor.

"Where were we Mrs. Brown?" he says as though the formality of calling me 'Mrs. Brown' somehow protects him now that a wall of nurse is standing between he and I.

He's still standing completely across the room though, and he doesn't look like he's going to come any closer.

I'm thinking to myself this guys a real chicken shit. He's a "doctor" for God's sake. He must see all kinds of crazy stuff.

"So, when I twist like this…" I say rotating my hip. This of course makes my zipper undo a little bit more.

There's no response. Nothing. Nada. Not even an

'*ahem*'! But when I look at him, I see a bead of sweat has formed on his forehead.

"Didn't you hear that?" I ask.

"Hear what?" he says.

"My hip," I say.

What? This guy's so damned afraid I'm going to drop my pants or something that he's completely forgotten why I'm here.

"Oh…No I didn't hear it," he says looking down at the floor.

"Well, maybe you should come a little closer, maybe put your hand right here so you can feel my crack." I say.

"Um," dribbles from his mouth as his face changes to a brighter shade of red as the words 'feel my crack' sinks in.

"DOCTOR, hellooooo…" I say, hoping to rein him back down from wherever his mind has drifted.

I glance at his groin just to make certain his pleasure center is still officially shut down.

"Oh! Yes, of course," he says.

But he still doesn't move.

Finally, Nurse Ratchet steps up to the plate for him and shuffles towards me. She pulls my pants down a little then puts her hand near my groin.

HOLY CRAP!

This woman should have 'Ice Queen' written on her nametag instead of...WHAT? This does not look like a Cindy.

Now, I know there are no rules about this, but there should be.

RULE #2: Medical practitioners should be required to warm up their hands or anything else that's going to come in contact with your body!

"Okay, do it again, *NOW*," she says. "I'll feel your crack for him."

I feel a little uncomfortable with the location of her hand, especially after noticing that she's not wearing a wedding band. And it's no consolation when I spot the badass tattoo peeking out of her short-sleeved uniform.

"Actually, if you put your hand on my back, you'll probably feel it better," I manage to spit out as I continue to adjust to the temperature of her paw.

"Are you telling me how to do my job, ma'am?"

OH NO YOU DIDN'T!

She doesn't know me well enough yet to pull the

'ma'am' card. (*to be continued in Volume II*).

OTHER BOOKS BY THE AUTHOR

DANCING WITH THE DEVIL
JACQUI BROWN

RECOVERY'S A BITCH
[AS IF MENOPAUSE ALONE WASN'T BAD ENOUGH!]
JACQUI BROWN

LAUGHING MY ASS OFF
~CLASSIC E JOKES~
(VOLUME I, II, III, IV)
JACQUI BROWN

IMAGINE WORDS
JACQUI BROWN

CPSIA information can be obtained at www.ICGtesting.com
Printed in the USA
LVOW01s1457271013

358781LV00012B/298/P

9 781475 202403